ASSISTING INDIVIDUALS IN CRISIS

4th Edition

George S. Everly, Jr., Ph.D., F.A.P.M.

The Johns Hopkins University
and
Loyola College in Maryland

INTERNATIONAL
CRITICAL
INCIDENT
STRESS
FOUNDATION

For more information, contact ICISF at:
3290 Pine Orchard Lane, Suite 106
Ellicott City, Maryland 21042
(410) 750-9600
(410) 750-9601 fax
web site: www.icisf.org
EMERGENCY (410) 313-2473

ISBN 0-9765815-2-3

DEDICATION

To all of those who dare to attempt to alleviate human suffering
one moment at a time.

TABLE
OF
CONTENTS

Note:

The contents of this workbook are provided as a set of general guidelines only. The course or workbook is not intended to be used as a self- help manual, nor as a substitute for psychotherapy or professional mental health guidance. When in doubt, always consult a licensed mental health professional. Similarly, this manual may not be used as a substitute for formal training, supervision, or field experience.

The content of this course may be emotionally distressing to some participants. Participants are encouraged to leave the training at any point should they find the material excessively distressing. The instructor will be available to participants during the training to discuss any adverse reactions to the course material, should this occur.

TOPICAL OUTLINE AND CORSE OBJECTIVES

ASSISTING INDIVIDUALS IN CRISIS
Topical Outline

Section One - Key Terms & Concepts

Section Two - Are You Listening?

Section Three - Crisis Communication Techniques

Section Four - Questions

ASSISTING INDIVIDUALS IN CRISIS
Topical Outline

Section Five - Psychological Reactions in Crisis

Section Six - Mechanisms of Action

Section Seven - Do No Harm!

Section Eight - The SAFER-Revised Model

Revised 10/2005

OBJECTIVES: Participants will...

1. Understand the natures & definitions of a psychological crisis and psychological crisis intervention.

2. Understand key issues and findings of evidence-based, and evidence-informed practice as it relates to psychological crisis intervention.

3. Understand the resistance, resiliency, recovery continuum.

OBJECTIVES: Participants will...

4. Understand the nature and definition of critical incident stress management and its role as a continuum of care.

5. Practice basic crisis communication techniques.

6. Be familiar with common psychological and behavioral crisis reactions, including empirically-derived predictors of posttraumatic stress disorder.

7. Understand the putative and empirically-derived mechanisms of action in psychological crisis intervention.

OBJECTIVES: Participants will...

8. Practice the SAFER-Revised model of individual psychological crisis intervention.

9. Understand how the SAFER-Revised model may be altered for suicide intervention.

10. Understand and discuss the risks of iatrogenic "harm" associated with psychological crisis intervention and will further discuss how to reduce those risks.

KEY TERMS AND CONCEPTS

Section
I

THE NEED

- Over 80% Americans will be exposed to a traumatic event (Breslau) About 9% of those exposed develop PTSD (40-70% IN RAPE, TORTURE) (Surgeon General, 1999)

- Disasters may create significant impairment in 40-50% of those exposed (Norris, 2001, SAMHSA)

THE NEED

- About 50% of disaster workers likely to develop significant distress (Myers & Wee, 2005)

- Terrorism likely to adversely impact majority of population (IOM, 2003); Ranges from ~ 40 - 90% (JHU, 2005)

- Dose response relationship with exposure

THE NEED

- PTSD Prevalence: 10 - 15% of Law Enforcement Personnel (see Everly & Mitchell, 1999)

- PTSD Prevalence: 10 - 30% of those in Fire Suppression (see Everly & Mitchell, 1999)

- PTSD Prevalence: 16% Vietnam Veterans (Nat PTSD Study)

THE NEED

➤ PTSD Prevalence: ~ 12% Iraq War Veterans (NEJM, 2004)

➤ As many as 45% of those directly exposed to mass disasters may develop PTSD or depression (North, et al., 1999, JAMA)

At the heart of any field of study or practice resides a basic vocabulary. The following definitions will set the stage for the material we will cover in this course.

DEFINITIONS

CRITICAL INCIDENTS are unusually challenging events that have the potential to create significant human DISTRESS and can overwhelm one's usual coping mechanisms.

Terrorism: A Special Case

Terrorism may be understood from several perspectives:

- From a law enforcement perspective, terrorism may be thought of as the premeditated and **unlawful use, or threatened use, of force or violence** as a coercive or punitive agent.

- From a military perspective, terrorism represents **war waged against civilians** (Carr, 2002).

- From a psychological/ behavioral perspective, terrorism represents **psychological warfare**. The psychoactively toxic mechanism inherent in terrorism is *demoralization*. Its behavioral corollary is **capitulation** (Everly & Castellano, 2005).

THE ICEBERG EFFECT OF TERRORISM (and disasters)… more psychological casualties than physical casualties…80/20 Effect?

(Holloway, et al., 1997, JAMA; DiGiovanni, 1999, Am. J. Psychiatry)

DEFINITIONS

The psychological DISTRESS in response to critical incidents such as emergencies, disasters, traumatic events, terrorism, or catastrophes is called a PSYCHOLOGICAL CRISIS

(Everly & Mitchell, 1999)

PSYCHOLOGICAL CRISIS

An acute RESPONSE to a trauma, disaster, or other critical incident wherein:

1. Psychological homeostasis (balance) is disrupted (increased stress)
2. One's usual coping mechanisms have failed
3. There is evidence of significant distress, **impairment**, dysfunction

(adapted from Caplan, 1964, *Preventive Psychiatry*)

DEFINITIONS

CRISIS INTERVENTION

A short-tem helping process.

Acute intervention designed to mitigate the crisis response.

Not psychotherapy.

CRISIS INTERVENTION

Goals: To foster natural resiliency through…

1. Stabilization
2. Symptom reduction
3. Return to adaptive functioning, or
4. Facilitation of access to continued care

(adapted from Caplan, 1964, *Preventive Psychiatry*)

IMPORTANT!
Crisis intervention targets the RESPONSE, not the EVENT, per se.

Thus, crisis intervention and disaster mental health interventions must be predicated upon assessment of need.

CRISIS INTERVENTION

Historical roots of current crisis intervention practices can be found

in military psychiatry, community mental health, and suicide intervention initiatives.

Foundations of Military "Crisis Intervention"

- WWI – 1916, *Postes de chirurgie d'urgence*, 66% returned to combat after 7 days treatment

- WWI – 1917, 1919, Thomas Salmon describes immediacy & proximity, i.e., "treatment within the sound of artillery"

Foundations of Military "Crisis Intervention"

❧ Sargant, W. (1942). Physical treatment of acute war neurosis. British Medical Journal, Nov 14, 1942, pp. 574-576: "Our most important finding has been the supreme need for immediate first aid treatment of the acute neurosis…"p 574)

❧ SLA Marshall (Island Victory, 1944) described the manner and value of group intervention via historical event reconstruction

---

Military foundations for crisis intervention have evolved since 1919:

❧ Proximity

❧ Immediacy

❧ Expectancy

And later added:

❧ Brevity

❧ Simplicity

ARTISS (Military Medicine, 1963)
Regarding war neurosis, removal of the soldier from the front "returned only five percent of such casualties to duty" (p. 1011). The treatment principles of immediacy, proximity, & expectancy were later applied and resulted in 70 to 80 percent of combat psychiatric casualties returning to duty.

KARDINER (Am. Hdbk. Psyc, 1959).

"Those on field duty found it to be most advantageous to the soldier, and to the army, to recognize exhaustion and the fear but not to remove the soldier to the rear" (p. 248). "By and large, the prognosis...varies directly with the time factor...The great issue...is not to permit the syndrome to become entrenched..." (p253).

KARDINER (Am. Hdbk. Psyc, 1959).

"The most effective implement is to keep alive the [causal] relation between the symptoms and the traumatic event" [as opposed to attributing symptoms to weakness in character] (p 254). In addition, Kardiner noted, to a significant degree, the soldier's expectation of outcome predicts recovery from war neurosis.

RESEARCH FINDINGS

LESSONS LEARNED FROM COMMUNITY MENTAL HEALTH

- Early Psychological Intervention may reduce the need for more intensive psyc services. (Langsley, Machotka, & Flomenhaft, 1971, Am J Psyc; Decker, & Stubblebine, 1972, Am J Psyc)

- Early Psychological Intervention may mitigate acute distress . (Bordow & Porritt, 1979, Soc Sci & Med; Bunn & Clarke, 1979, Br. J Med. Psychol;Campfield & Hills, 2001, JTS; Everly, et al., 1999, Stress Med; Flannery & Everly, 2004, Aggression & Violent Beh.)

LESSONS LEARNED FROM COMMUNITY MENTAL HEALTH

- Early psychological Intervention may reduce ETOH use. (Deahl, et al, 2000, Br J Med Psychol; Boscarino, et al., 2005)

Not all mental health professionals agree that crisis intervention / disaster psychological intervention is useful.

Note: The term "debriefing" is often used as a synonym for crisis intervention / disaster mental health / early psychological intervention.

Concern over perceived indiscriminant use of psychological crisis intervention has led to recommendations to wait 1-3 months post event before initiating formal psychological intervention using 4-12 sessions of Cognitive Behavioral Therapy (CBT).

[see Friedman, M., Foa, E., & Charney, D. (2003). Toward evidence-based early intervention for acutely traumatized adults and children. Biological Psychiatry, 53, 765-768.]

Concerns have been fueled
by publication of the
Cochrane Reviews…

Major concern over the applicability of
early psychological intervention arose
largely from the Cochrane Reviews (1998,
2002).
Other negative reviews (van Emmerick, et
al., 2002; McNally, et al., 2003) were based
largely upon Cochrane data sets, and
subsequent theoretical speculation as to
potential mechanisms of pathogenic
iatrogenesis.

COCHRANE REVIEW (2002)

- "Debriefing" = 11 RCT studies of 1:1
  counseling with medical / surgical patients,
  "loosely based" upon outdated (1983) model

- "Debriefing" = "single session individual
  debriefing did not reduce psychological
  distress nor prevent PTSD"

COCHRANE REVIEW (2002)

➢ 3 studies showed worsening of symptoms

➢ The authors conclude: "We are unable to comment on the use of group debriefing, nor the use of debriefing after mass traumas."

The Debriefing "Controversy" and Crisis Intervention: A Review of Lexical and Substantive Issues

George S. Everly, Jr., Ph.D. and Jeffrey T. Mitchell, Ph.D.

ABSTRACT: *Despite a long and rich history as a specialty within applied mental health, crisis intervention has, within recent years, been the target of criticism. Singled out for specific criticism has been the intervention referred to as "debriefing." Some authors have not only challenged its effectiveness but have raised the specter that it may cause significant harm. While superficially such arguments appear to have merit, closer scrutiny reveals an antiquated interpretation of even the most fundamental of terms and concepts inextricably intertwined with research based upon applications contrary to the most recent principles, prescriptions, and protocols regarding clinical use. A review of research based upon more extant formulations reveals many crisis intervention practices, including the Critical Incident Stress Debriefing model of "debriefing" and the Critical Incident Stress Management (CISM) model of crisis intervention to be highly clinically effective, indeed. This paper will review the terms and concepts which serve as the foundation of the field of crisis intervention, while subsequently reviewing key research investigations addressing its efficacy. It may be that outcome research directed toward assessing the effectiveness of crisis intervention can prosper from following trails blazed by psychotherapy researchers. The parallels seem striking. It may be that outcome research in crisis intervention (and "debriefing") needs to now focus upon "who" does crisis intervention, to "whom," and in "what specific situations," so as to maximize outcome associated with this clinically effective tool [International Journal of Emergency Mental Health, 2000, 2(4), 211-225].*

KEY WORDS: debriefing, emergency mental health, crisis intervention, Critical Incident Stress Debriefing (CISD), Critical Incident Stress Management (CISM)

The words we choose to express a thought or capture a concept not only represent a medium of communication, but they affect the opinions we hold, the rhetoric we proffer, even the "science" we teach. Psycholinguistic scholar Benjamin Lee Whorf postulated, in the formulation of what was to be known as the Whorfian hypothesis of linguistic relativity, that words have the power of shaping cognitive processes. In effect, words can shape how we think and the beliefs we hold. The poet T.S. Eliot once wrote that words decay with imprecision. It was George Engel, one of the pioneers in the field of psychosomatic medicine, who once said that a substantive issue in rational discourse is the need to use terms consistently. Surely no discussion of issues, no debate about theory or research, nor any conduct associated with inquiry regarding effective practice can be meaningful, nor anything but pseudo-science, without a definition of, and agreement upon, fundamental terms and concepts. Indeed, the foundation of all scientific inquiry is reliability. Unfortunately, the field of emergency mental health, and crisis intervention per se, has been made unnecessarily complicated because of an imprecise and unreliable utilization of even the most fundamental of terms. Although the field enjoys a long and rich history, recently some terms have become distorted from their original formulations or current

George S. Everly, Jr., Ph.D., Loyola College in Maryland and The Johns Hopkins University, and Jeffrey T. Mitchell, Ph.D., Emergency Health Services at the University of Maryland Baltimore County. Address correspondence concerning this article to: George S. Everly, Jr., Ph.D., 702 Severnside Ave., Severna Park, MD 21146

Note: This paper contains elements written for the American Psychological Association's Consensus Conference on the Mental Health Needs of Emergency Medical Services for Children (EMSC) Providers, Washington, D.C., October 5-6, 2000

evolutionary representations. Most recently, for example, Kenardy (2000) has stated, "Psychological debriefing is broadly defined as a set of procedures including counseling and the giving of information aimed at preventing psychological morbidity and aiding recovery after a traumatic event" (p. 1032). This definition of psychological debriefing while anchored in the historical literature (Mitchell, 1983) is clearly: a) not conducive to easily replicated empirical investigations due to a lack of specificity and standardization, and b) in juxtaposition to more recent formulations which have evolved over the last 25 years wherein the term "debriefing" refers to a standardized group crisis intervention. This paper will first review some of the terms that are fundamental to the practice of crisis intervention and the overall provision of acute psychological support. By reviewing such lexical foundations, some of the "differences of opinion" that exist in the field of crisis intervention may be better illuminated. Secondly, this paper will review empirically derived evidence as to the clinical efficacy of crisis intervention.

A Review of Basic Terms

"Crisis." A crisis may be thought of as a response to some aversive situation, manifest or anticipated, wherein:

1) psychological homeostasis (equilibrium) is disrupted;
2) one's usual coping mechanisms have failed to reestablish homeostasis; and,
3) there is evidence of functional distress or impairment (Caplan, 1961, 1964; Everly & Mitchell, 1999).

"Critical incident" is a term which refers to an event which is outside the usual range of experience and challenges one's ability to cope. The critical incident has the potential to lead to a crisis condition by overwhelming one's usual psychological defenses and coping mechanisms.

"Crisis intervention" is the natural operational corollary of the conceptualization of the term crisis. Consistent with the defining formulations of Caplan (1961, 1964), crisis intervention may be thought of as urgent and acute psychological "first aid," the hallmarks of which are:

1) immediacy, i.e., early intervention
2) proximity, i.e., intervention within close physical proximity to the acute crisis manifestation
3) expectancy, i.e., the expectation of the recipient is

that of an acute problem-focused intervention
4) brevity, i.e., the intervention will be short in the totality of its duration often lasting only one to three contacts, and
5) simplicity, i.e., simple, directive interventions seem to be the most useful, whereas, complex interventions which require a) the interpretation of unconscious motives, b) paradoxical intention, or c) confrontation should usually be avoided.

The goals of crisis intervention are:

1) stabilization, i.e., cessation of escalating distress thus keeping the response from worsening
2) mitigation of acute signs and symptoms of distress, dysfunction, or impairment, and,
3) restoration of adaptive independent functioning, if possible; or,
4) facilitation of access to a higher level of care (Everly & Mitchell, 1999). By virtue of the inclusion of this aspect of the definition, we render moot the notion that some individuals may be "too severely affected" to benefit from crisis intervention. The final obligation of the crisis interventionist is to provide for, or facilitate access to, services which will assist in the restoration of adaptive independent functioning in the wake of a traumatic, or critical, incident.

"Critical Incident Stress Debriefing" (CISD). Critical Incident Stress Debriefing (CISD) is actually a proper noun (Mitchell, 1983). CISD refers to one form, or model, of *group* crisis intervention, sometimes generically referred to as group psychological debriefing. As group psychotherapy is to individual psychotherapy, the group CISD is to individual crisis intervention. More specifically, CISD represents one author's approach (Mitchell & Everly, 1997) to group crisis intervention. CISD represents a highly structured form of group crisis intervention and represents a discussion of the traumatic, or critical, incident. The most current CISD model of psychological debriefing contains seven distinct stages, or phases. The CISD typically takes 1.5 to 3.0 hours to conduct. It is most commonly conducted 2 to 14 days after a critical incident. In cases of mass disasters, the CISD is not recommended until three to four weeks post disaster. The expressed intention of the CISD is to provide some facilitation of the process of psychological "closure" upon the traumatic, or critical, incident (i.e., the facilitation of the reconstruction process). When closure is not possible, the CISD may serve as a useful mechanism for psychological triage so as to

identify those who will need more advanced care. The CISD was originally formulated for use with emergency services personnel who were potential vicarious victims of traumas and critical incidents (Mitchell, 1983), but has been used with primary victims in a wide variety of setting including schools, businesses, industrial settings, the airline industry, and mass disasters. Historically, CISD represents the oldest and most commonly used non-military form of psychological debriefing which uses a standardized structure. But the roots of group debriefing actually date back to the military applications during World War II. Nevertheless, CISD is the root from whence the currently used generic term "debriefing," in the psychological sense, was originally derived. Its originator, Jeffrey T. Mitchell, Ph.D., contends that CISD was never intended to be a "stand-alone" intervention, nor a substitute for psychotherapy (Mitchell & Everly, 1997). Rather, the CISD is one form of group crisis intervention which represents one component within a larger crisis intervention program referred to as Critical Incident Stress Management (CISM; Everly & Mitchell, 1999).

A relatively new term, that has emerged in the crisis intervention literature within the last decade, is *"Critical Incident Stress Management."* (CISM; Everly & Mitchell, 1999). CISM refers to an integrated, multi-component crisis intervention system (Everly & Mitchell, 1999), in contradistinction to the singular crisis intervention formulations of the past. The CISM system consists of a multitude of crisis intervention technologies which span the crisis spectrum from the pre-crisis phase, through the acute crisis phase, to the post-crisis phase.

The historical evolution of the CISM system has, unfortunately, created considerable semantic confusion. Initially, Mitchell (1983) authored a paper on crisis intervention as it applied to emergency services personnel wherein the Critical Incident Stress Debriefing (CISD) process was described. Mitchell (1983) stated, "The CISD is an organized approach to the management of stress responses in emergency services. It entails either an individual or group meeting…"(p. 37). He went on to describe a multi-component crisis intervention approach which included a small group crisis intervention referred to as a formal critical incident stress debriefing (CISD). Considerable semantic confusion resulted from Mitchell's use of the term CISD to denote more than one thing: 1) the overarching framework for his crisis intervention system (CISD), 2) a specific six-phase small group discussion process ("formal"

CISD), and 3) the optional follow-up intervention (follow-up CISD). As a result, the current literature is plagued with references to "individual debriefings," and the perpetuated, but erroneous, notion that the CISD group discussion was intended to be a stand-alone, or "one-off" intervention. In an effort to rectify the lexical discord and expand the original formulations, the term Critical Incident Stress Management (CISM) was chosen as the term to denote the overarching, multi-component approach to crisis intervention, thus replacing the term CISD as it was originally used in that context. The term CISD is now used exclusively to denote what has become a specific seven-phase group crisis intervention process.

The program in TABLE 1 is a prototypic CISM system. It is an integrated, multi-componential system that is designed to be a "comprehensive" intervention system. The formulation offered herein is considered comprehensive because it consists of multiple crisis intervention components which functionally span the entire temporal spectrum of a crisis. Interventions range from the pre-crisis phase through the acute crisis phase, and into the post-crisis phase. The extant formulation is also considered comprehensive in that it consists of interventions which may be applied to individuals, small functional groups, large groups, families, organizations, and even communities. The core components of the program are defined below:

1) Pre-incident preparation. Pre-incident preparation may be thought of as a form of psychological "immunization." The goal is to strengthen potential vulnerabilities and enhance psychological resiliency in individuals who may be at risk for psychological crises and/or psychological traumatization. One important aspect of pre-incident preparation is the provision of information. Sir Francis Bacon once noted, "Information itself is power." Many crises and traumas result from a violation of expectancy, thus setting realistic expectations serves to protect against violated assumptions. But pre-incident preparation also consists of behavioral response preparation and rehearsal. This includes familiarization with common stressors, stress management education, stress resistance training, and crisis mitigation training for line personnel as well as management.

2) Disaster or large scale crisis intervention programs including *demobilizations, staff advisement, and crisis management briefings (CMB).* The demobilization is an opportunity for temporary psychological "decompression"

Table 1: Critical Incident Stress Management (CISM): The Core Components
(Adapted from: Everly and Mitchell, 1999)

	INTERVENTION	TIMING	ACTIVATION	GOAL	FORMAT
1.	Pre-crisis preparation.	Pre-crisis phase.	Crisis anticipation.	Set expectations, Improve coping, Stress management.	Groups/ Organizations.
2a	Demobilizations & staff consultation (rescuers).	Shift disengagement.	Event driven.	To inform and consult, allow psychological decompression. Stress management.	Large groups/ Organizations.
2b.	Crisis Management Briefing (CMB) (civilians, schools, business).	Anytime post-crisis.			
3.	Defusing.	Post-crisis (within 12 hours).	Usually symptom driven.	Symptom mitigation. Possible closure. Triage.	Small groups.
4.	Critical Incident Stress Debriefing (CISD)	Post-crisis (1 to 10 days; 3-4 weeks mass disasters)	Usually symptom driven; can be event driven.	Facilitate psychological closure. Sx mitigation. Triage.	Small groups.
5.	Individual crisis intervention (1:1).	Anytime, Anywhere.	Symptom driven	Symptom mitigation. Return to function, if possible. Referral, if needed.	Individuals.
6.	Pastoral Crisis Intervention.	Anytime, Anywhere.	Whenever needed.	Provide spiritual, faith-based support.	Individuals/ Groups.
7a.	Family CISM.	Anytime.	Either symptom driven or event driven.	Foster support & communications. Symptom mitigation. Closure, if possible. Referral, if needed.	Families/ Organizations.
7b.	Organizational consultation.				
8.	Follow-up/Referral.	Anytime.	Usually symptom driven.	Assess mental status. Access higher level of care, if needed.	Individual/ Family.

[From : Everly, G. & Mitchell, J. (1999) Critical Incident Stress Management (CISM): A New Era and Standard of Care in Crisis Intervention. Ellicott City, MD: Chevron Publishing.]

immediately after exposure to a critical incident. This technique was originally developed for use by emergency services personnel. Staff advisement refers to the provision of psychological consultations to command staff (emergency services personnel, military, disaster response teams), as well as management personnel in business and industrial settings. The crisis management briefing (CMB) refers to a four-step crisis intervention for large groups of individuals (up to 300 at one time). The CMB is ideal for school crises, business and industrial crises, community violence and mass disasters (see Everly, 2000a; Newman, 2000).

3) *Defusing.* This is a 3-phase, 45 minute, structured small group discussion provided within hours of a crisis for purposes of assessment, triaging, and acute symptom mitigation. In some cases, the defusing may do much to foster psychological closure after a critical incident.

4) *Critical Incident Stress Debriefing (CISD)* refers to the 7-phase, structured group discussion, usually provided 1 to 14 days post crisis (although in mass disasters may be used 3 weeks or more post incident), and designed to mitigate acute symptoms, assess the need for follow-up, and if possible provide a sense of post-crisis psychological closure (Mitchell & Everly, 1997). In fact one of the great utilities of the CISD appears to be facilitating psychological reconstruction. Due to its structure, the CISD may take up to two to three hours to complete. The CISD will sometimes be used subsequent to the crisis management briefing and the defusing. The CISD is almost always followed by intervention on an individual basis with those individuals who require it. Referral for more formal mental health intervention may then follow.

5) *One-on-one crisis intervention/counseling* or psychological support throughout the full range of the crisis spectrum (this is the most frequently used of the CISM interventions). Typically, this form of intervention consists of 1 to 3 contacts with an individual who is in crisis. Each contact may last 15 minutes to more than 2 hours depending upon the nature and severity of the crisis. Although flexible and efficient, this form of crisis intervention lacks the added advantage of group process. Because of its extreme time-limited nature, it is especially important with this intervention as with all crisis interventions, to avoid using paradoxical interventions, interpretation of unconscious processes, or confrontational techniques (see Everly & Mitchell, 1999).

6) *Pastoral crisis intervention* (Everly, 2000b), more than ministerial or chaplaincy services, represents the integration of traditional crisis intervention with pastoral-based support services. In addition to traditional crisis intervention tools, pastoral crisis intervention may employ scriptural education, prayer (personal, conjoint, intercessory), rituals and sacraments, and the unique ethos of the pastoral crisis interventionist. A specialized form of crisis intervention, pastoral crisis intervention may not be suited for all persons or all circumstances, nevertheless, it represents a valuable addition the comprehensive CISM matrix.

7) *Family crisis intervention, as well as, organizational consultation* represent crisis intervention at the systems level. Both family and organizational crisis intervention, when done most effectively will possess proactive (pre-crisis) and reactive elements.

8) *Follow-up and referral mechanisms for assessment and treatment,* if necessary. No crisis intervention system is complete without the recognition that some critical incidents are so toxic by their very nature, that they will require a more intense and formalized intervention, perhaps even psychotropic medications. Therefore it is important to build into any crisis intervention system, a mechanism for follow-up assessment and treatment for those individuals for whom acute crisis intervention techniques prove insufficient. An important aspect of this element is the existence of a set of principles or guidelines for psychological triage (see Everly, 1999).

TABLE 1 further describes this crisis intervention system. Specific guidelines for these interventions may be found in Flannery (1998), Mitchell and Everly (1997), and Everly and Mitchell (1999).

It appears clear that one of the most potentially traumatogenetic critical incidents is the serious injury to, or death of, children (Dyregrov & Mitchell, 1992; Figley, 1995). Athey and her colleagues (Athey et al., 1997) specifically recommend the comprehensive CISM program for providers of emergency medical services to children. They conclude, "Institutionalizing and normalizing CISM for both large-scale and small events will help improve the emergency care system" (Athey et al., 1997, p. 467). Similarly, Shannon (1991) has commented upon the value of having this crisis intervention system available for those who provide emergency medical care, especially involving children. But multi-faceted CISM programs have been implemented in other traumatogenetic venues, as well.

A review of exemplary crisis intervention programs reveals that they tend to be integrated and multi-componential in nature. Multi-component CISM crisis intervention programs appear to be emerging as the recommended industry standard, a virtual standard of care (Everly & Mitchell, 1999). Variations of the CISM model have been adopted by numerous and diverse organizations in a wide variety of workplace settings including the Federal Aviation Administration (FAA), the United States Air Force (1997 Air Force Instruction 44153), the United States Coast Guard (1999 COMDTINST 1754.3), the U.S. Secret Service, the Federal Bureau of Investigation (FBI), the Bureau of Alcohol, Tobacco, and Firearms (ATF), the Airline Pilots' Association (ALPA), the Swedish National Police, the Association of Icelandic Rescue Teams, the Australian Navy, the Australian Army, and the Massachusetts Department of Mental Health. Even the Department of Defense (1999 Directive 6490.5) has mandated attention be given to the prevention of combat stress reactions. In 1996, Occupational Safety and Health Administration (OSHA) document 3148-1996 recommended the implementation of comprehensive violence/crisis intervention programs in social service and healthcare settings. In 1998, OSHA 3153-1998 further recommended multi-component crisis intervention programs for late-night retail stores.

Research Findings and the Debriefing "Controversy"

The issue of the effectiveness of crisis intervention first emerged in the clinical literature in the 1960s. Artiss (1963) reported that the psychotherapeutic elements of immediacy, proximity, and expectancy had been employed successfully in military psychiatry to reduce psychiatric morbidity and increase return to combat rates for American soldiers. Solomon & Benbenishty (1986) confirmed with Israeli soldiers what Artiss had observed with the United States military. These authors concluded that early intervention, proximal intervention, and the role of expectation were each associated with positive outcome. Parad & Parad (1968) reviewed 1,656 social work cases and found crisis-oriented intervention to be effective in reducing florid psychiatric complaints and in improving patients' ability to cope with stress. Langsley, Machotka, & Flomenhaft (1971) followed 300 psychiatric patients randomly assigned to inpatient treatment or family crisis intervention groups. The crisis intervention group was found to be superior in reducing the need for subsequent hospital admissions at 6 and 18 month intervals. A similar finding was recorded by Decker & Stubblebine (1972) using a single group 2.5 year longitudinal design. Finally, it was Bordow & Porritt (1979) who initially demonstrated, through randomized experimental design, that multicomponent crisis intervention was superior to single crisis tactics. Empirical evidence such as this argues for the effectiveness of early intervention, crisis-based psychological support tactics, while at the same time arguing against the attribution of psychotherapeutic exclusivity to traditional individual or group psychotherapy.

On first appearance, the issue of the effectiveness of psychological "debriefing" appears a more perplexing issue. Yet, careful scrutiny of relevant literature yields greater insight into this controversy. It may well be that the controversy surrounding debriefing is more lexical than substantive.

Initial concern over the effectiveness of psychological debriefings arose in the relevant literature with the publication of two Australian studies. McFarlane (1988) reported on the longitudinal course of posttraumatic morbidity in the wake of bush fires. One aspect of the study found that acute posttraumatic stress was predicted by avoidance of thinking about problems, property loss, and not attending undefined forms of psychological debriefings. However, chronic variations of posttraumatic stress disorder were best predicted by premorbid, non-event related factors, such as a family history of psychiatric disorders, concurrent avoidance and neuroticism, and a tendency not to confront conflicts. The delayed onset posttraumatic stress group not only had higher premorbid neuroticism scores, and greater property loss, but also attended the undefined debriefings. While these factors, when submitted to discriminant function analysis, only resulted in the correct identification of 53% of the delayed onset group, this study is often reported as evidence for lack of effectiveness of debriefings.

The second of the early negative outcome studies was that of Kenardy et al., (1996). Kenardy's investigation purported to assess the effectiveness of stress debriefings for 62 "debriefed helpers" compared to 133 who were apparently not debriefed subsequent to an earthquake in New Castle, Australia. This study is often cited as evidence for the ineffectiveness of debriefings, yet the authors state, "we were not able to influence the availability or nature of the debriefing. . . (p. 39). They continue, "It was assumed that all subjects in this study who reported having been debriefed did in fact receive posttrauma debriefing. However, there was no standardization of debriefing services. . ."(p.47).

These rather remarkable epistemological revelations by the authors have failed to deter critics of the "debriefing" process, whatever the term may mean.

Unfortunately, those who cite these investigations as "evidence" of the lack of effectiveness of "psychological debriefings" appear to have neglected the immutable empirical reality that failure to insure the standardization and reliability of the independent variable (debriefing) renders the results of the investigations unintelligible, ungeneralizable, and certainly not supportive of the null hypothesis, as some would contend. The sine qua non of research is internal validity; unfortunately, these studies possess no such validity as it pertains to the evaluation of the effectiveness of CISD.

Perhaps the greatest contention regarding the use of debriefings has arisen from reviews constructed by Wessely, Rose, & Bisson (1997), sometimes referred to as the Cochrane Report, and by Rose & Bisson (1998). These reviews are held out to be methodologically robust because they employ only investigations using randomization. The primary investigations which qualified for inclusion are discussed below:

1) Bisson, Jenkins, Alexander, & Bannister (1997) randomly assigned 110 patients with severe burns to either a "debriefing" group or a control group. The clinical standard *group* debriefing was abandoned for an *individual* adaptation. The goal of the randomization was not met in that the "debriefed" individuals had more severe burns and greater financial problems than the non-debriefed individuals, thus direct comparison was inappropriate. These variables were later associated with poorer outcome. The "debriefed" group had more severe traumatic stress scores at 13 months. Despite the lack of equivalent groups and the failure to follow standard clinical protocols for group debriefings, these authors contend that the results cast serious doubt upon the utility of debriefings.

2) Hobbs, Mayou, Harrison, & Worlock (1996) performed a randomized trial of debriefings for 106 (54 debriefed; 52 control) motor vehicle accident victims. Once again randomization failed to achieve equivalent groups for comparison in that the individuals who were debriefed had more severe injuries and spent more days in the hospital. Both factors predicted poorer psychological outcome. Similarly, the clinical standard group process was abandoned so as to employ individual debriefings. The individuals receiving the debriefings had higher traumatic stress scores

at follow-up. These data have been used to argue that debriefing may be injurious, yet the actual traumatic stress scores were not in a clinical range at any time, and the overall change went from 15.13 to 15.97 (clinical ranges begin around 26). Such a change has no clinical significance whatsoever, and therefore cannot be construed as harmful. In a 4-year longitudinal follow-up investigation, Mayou, Ehlers, and Hobbs (2000) found the intervention group (individualized debriefings) remained symptomatic. Once again, however, the group debriefing process was not used, and the debriefing was used in a stand-alone manner (contrary to a multi-component prescription including follow-up). It seems a non-sequitur to conclude that psychological debriefing is ineffective and to further conclude that it is inappropriate for trauma patients when the debriefing process was individualized, as opposed to the group format, and when the debriefing was taken out of its prescribed multi-component context and applied to medical patients. The internal validity of these two investigations seems suspect at best, further, it seems impossible to generalize from these studies to any other debriefing protocols.

3) Lee, Slade, & Lygo (1996) assessed the effectiveness of individual debriefing on women following miscarriages. No significant changes were attributed to debriefings. In a more recent variation, Small et al. (2000) used "debriefing" subsequent to operative childbirth (Caesarean, forceps, or vacuum delivery). Once again individual debriefing was employed, as opposed to group debriefing. The debriefing took place prior to hospital discharge, while the psychological assessment took place at six months post childbirth. Unfortunately, the debriefing process, as operationalized in this study, was not specifically described. The reported results indicated that 94% of the women in the debriefing group found the debriefing either "helpful" or "very helpful" (n = 437/463). The intervention was found to be ineffective on the targeted symptoms of depression, as would be predicted. Debriefing is not a substitute for psychotherapy. Nevertheless, the authors surprisingly conclude this study fails to support the utility of debriefings.

4) Bordow & Porritt (1979) assessed the effectiveness of a multicomponent CISM-like crisis intervention on three groups of motor vehicle accident victims. The control group received no intervention, the second group received a one-session individual assessment/intervention, while the third group received the same as the second group plus 2-10 hours of crisis intervention. Results indicated a positive dose-

response relationship with intervention.

5) Bunn & Clarke (1979) conducted an experimental evaluation of brief intervention on anxiety symptoms for the relatives of seriously ill hospital patients. The intervention consisted of about 20 minutes of crisis counseling in which subjects received information, psychological support, and an opportunity to vent. Subjects were randomly assigned to experimental and control conditions. Results were supportive of the assumption that brief crisis counseling is an effective anxiolytic.

The results of these oft-cited reviews appear self-evident. First, none of these studies actually assessed the effectiveness of the international clinical standard in debriefing, the CISD model of debriefing. Therefore, they lack generalizability, specifically to CISD. Their lack of precise refinement of the independent variables make any pursuit of external validity difficult, at best, and would seem to restrict the utility of their findings to the idiosyncratic nature of their unique interventions. Therefore, rather than support the notion that group debriefings are ineffectual and may be harmful, these data would appear to support a very different set of conclusions.

First, these studies would appear to support the conclusion that clinicians should use caution implementing a group crisis intervention protocol with individuals singularly (Busuttil & Busuttil, 1995). Obviously, none of the therapeutic elements of group process (Yalom, 1970) are available to be used when a group protocol is employed one patient at a time. This would appear similar to attempting group psychotherapy protocols with individual psychotherapy patients.

Secondly, these findings would suggest caution with the use of individualized psychological crisis intervention tactics with primary medical patients within minimal temporal distance from their medical stressors, or with primary medical patients with ongoing medical stressors. Turnbull, Busuttil, and Pittman (1997) argue that such applications are inappropriate due to the timing of the intervention and the nature of the patients' crisis event or trauma. As a crisis intervention tactic, group debriefing is best suited for acute situational crisis responses. Debriefings are certainly not a substitute for psychotherapy, psychotropic medication, analgesics, or psychological rehabilitation.

Thirdly, the studies which used debriefing absent a positive outcome appeared to use the debriefing as a stand-alone intervention, outside of the prescribed multi-faceted CISM-like context (Everly & Mitchell, 1999). Kraus (1997) argues that debriefing should not be a stand-alone intervention, in agreement with Everly and Mitchell (1999) and the British Psychological Society (1990).

Fourth, given these admonitions, these findings appear to support the implementation of individual crisis counseling (Bunn & Clarke, 1979), and multi-component CISM-like interventions (Bordow & Porritt, 1979), as suggested earlier in this review. Unfortunately, no conclusions regarding group debriefings, in general, or CISD, in specific, can be made from these data (Everly & Mitchell, 1999; Robinson & Mitchell, 1995; Dyregrov, 1998).

To paraphrase the philosopher/ psychologist William James, "To disprove the assertion that all crows are black, one need only find one crow that is white!" Therefore, to disprove the assertion that all debriefings are ineffectual, one need only find one debriefing that is effective!

In support of debriefings, but specifically the CISD model of group psychological crisis intervention, we find several investigations: Robinson & Mitchell, (1993, 1995) with emergency medical services personnel; Nurmi (1999) with rescue personnel in the wake of the sinking of the Estonia; Wee et al., (1999) with emergency medical technicians subsequent to the Los Angeles riots; Bohl (1991) with police; Chemtob et al. (1997) with healthcare providers subsequent to Hurricane Iniki; and Jenkins (1996) with emergency medical personnel in the wake of a mass shooting. All of these investigations offer varying degrees of evidence for the effectiveness of the CISD intervention. In each of the studies cited, emergency services or other healthcare personnel were the recipients of the CISD intervention. Each of these studies, however, may be criticized for their lack of randomized subject assignment. However, four of the aforementioned studies possessed a static control condition, while one possessed a time-lagged control. These research designs are known to be vulnerable to selection, mortality, and maturation as threats to internal validity and the selection-intervention interaction threat to external validity (Campbell & Stanley, 1963). In order to partially compensate for the vulnerabilities and derive greater insight from their collective findings, Everly and Boyle (1999) subsequently meta-analyzed five of the aforementioned studies possessing control conditions. Perhaps the greatest singular value of randomization is the protection against systematic experimental error. One of the advantages of meta-analysis is that through combining investigations of diverse investigators using diverse subject populations in diverse naturalistic settings, the researcher is provided a large subject pool that is minimally vulnerable to systematic error, i.e., a similar goal as randomization. The results of the meta-analysis found cumulative evidence suggesting that the CISD is, indeed, clinically effective across applications (Everly & Boyle, 1999). This meta-analytic investigation revealed statistical sufficiency far in excess of that required to demonstrate reliability of the clinical effect ($Nfs_n=35$, $Nfs_o=91$). Most recently Watchorn (2000) has shown that group debriefings serve to prevent the development of PTSD. More specifically, the author concludes that peritraumatic dissociation predicts long-term impairment, but for those who dissociated, subsequent debriefings were associated with less impairment. Similarly, Deahl et al. (2000), in the only randomized investigation of the CISD model of debriefing, found CISD effective in reducing alcohol use and symptoms of anxiety, depression, and PTSD. This investigation was conducted with 106 British soldiers involved in a United Nations' peacekeeping mission. Soldiers were randomly assigned to a debriefing condition or a no debriefing condition. In addition, all soldiers received an Operational Stress Training Package. At the 6-month follow-up, the debriefed group evidenced a lower prevalence of alcohol use and lower scores on psychometrically assessed anxiety, depression, PTSD symptoms. Thus current evidence is compellingly supportive of the CISD model of debriefing as a means of mitigating adverse psychological responses to critical incidents and even more severe traumatic events. But it should be kept in mind that debriefings were not designed to be a stand-alone intervention. Rather, as noted earlier, the British Psychological Society (1990) and Mitchell and Everly (1997; Everly & Mitchell, 1999) argue that crisis intervention should be multi-faceted. Crisis intervention should be a multi-component endeavor, a fact that is often forgotten in actual practice.

The effectiveness of integrated multi-component CISM programs has now been suggested through thoughtful qualitative analyses (Everly, Flannery & Mitchell, 2000; Everly & Mitchell, 1999; Miller, 1999; Dyregrov, 1997, 1998 1999; Mitchell & Everly, 1997), as well as through empirical investigations, and even meta-analyses (Flannery, 1998; Flannery, Penk, & Corrigan, 1999; Flannery et al., 1995; Flannery et al., 1998; Flannery et al., 2000; Mitchell, Schiller, Everly, & Eyler, 1999; Everly, Flannery, & Eyler, in press, Flannery, Everly, & Eyler, 2000; Western Management Consultants, 1996). Flannery's ASAP program is an exemplary CISM crisis intervention approach (Flannery, 1998, 1999a, 1999b, 1999c) used in hospitals, clinics, and schools. Research has consistently shown the ASAP program to be an effective crisis intervention, but ASAP is curiously seldom cited in reviews of crisis intervention. A recent meta-analysis of five ASAP studies found the Cohen's d meta-analytic coefficient to be in excess of 3.00 showing a highly significant and powerful clinical effect (Flannery, Everly, & Eyler, 2000). Most recently, Flannery (in press) has reviewed 14 peer reviewed publications on the ASAP CISM intervention. The review, spanning ten years of published data supports the conclusion that the ASAP CISM intervention model is an effective model of crisis intervention. These data would appear to further serve as justification for the establishment of CISM programs within high-risk occupational groups. These data represent the longest ongoing investigation of a standardized model of crisis intervention available in written record. Richards (1999) has demonstrated the relative superiority of the multi-component CISM compared to the singular CISD, consistent with expectations. In the latest and largest meta-analytic investigation of CISM, Everly, Flannery, & Eyler (in press) found a Cohen's d of 3.1 and a fail-safe number of 792 when combining eight investigations. These findings are indicative of a powerful clinical effect exerted by the CISM programs.

Critics of CISD and/or CISM point out that the investigations supporting such forms of crisis intervention are mostly of a quasi-experimental nature, which is curious in that the review above revealed that the investigations which call into question the effectiveness of crisis intervention, generally, and CISD or CISM, specifically, reveals the lack of a clearly defined and standardized intervention (independent variable). Indeed, many studies which purport to assess debriefings failed to actually employ the standardized group CISD or integrated CISM protocols. As Richards (1999) has noted, the research investigations which most challenge the effectiveness of group crisis interventions sacrifice internal content validity in order to achieve experimental control. In this process, the outcomes are rendered inapplicable to a genre of crisis intervention technologies, yet are more a commentary of the ill-defined experimental interventions that were actually employed and/ or the clinical skill of the interventionists themselves. The standardized multi-component CISM approach (Everly & Mitchell, 1999) to crisis intervention is designed to remedy this short-coming by offering an intervention "manual" of sorts which can enhance the content validity of the independent variable as well as the external validity.

Clearly, randomized research designs which can assess the effectiveness of crisis intervention are certainly welcomed, if they can be instituted without sacrificing internal content validity. It was noted earlier that CISM has been submitted to meta-analytic scrutiny and initially found to be effective on the basis of empirical investigations (Everly, Flannery, & Eyler, in press; Flannery, Everly, & Eyler, 2000). Although the component investigations were quasi-experimental, they are not without epistemological value for several reasons. First, the use of such designs, even single case designs, can be useful in contributing meaningful data to the conduct of inquiry (Herson & Barlow, 1976; Blampied, 2000). Second, faithful adherence to the standardized protocols (specifically CISD or CISM) serves as the foundation of internal validity and serves to enhance specified external validity. Third, the use of meta-analysis serves to diminish the likelihood of systematic error across the participant investigations and compensate for specific threats to internal validity. Fourth, the use of meta-analysis with diverse recipient groups also serves to enhance the external validity of the meta-analytic findings supporting the effectiveness of CISD and CISM. Fifth, the use of combinatorial meta-analytic strategies increases the power of the findings by increasing the sample population thus increasing the credibility of the subsequent findings (Seligman, 1995). Nevertheless, randomized designs are certainly welcomed in the future.

Conclusion

Swanson and Carbon (1989) writing for the American Psychiatric Association Task Force Report on Treatment of Psychiatric Disorders state, "Crisis intervention is a proven approach to helping in the pain of an emotional crisis" (p. 2520). While there is a compelling logic to support the notion of early psychological intervention subsequent to a critical incident, while there is evidence to support the use of CISD and CISM, continued empirical validation and clinical refinement are worthy pursuits for the future. Although not supported by applicable empiricism, there remains among some researchers a seemingly dogmatic belief that crisis intervention, CISD, and/or CISM represent potentially harmful interventions. One must always acknowledge the risk associated with human healthcare. This is true in the practice of medicine, nursing, surgery, psychotherapy, and even crisis intervention. But, it seems the most prudent approach to this issue lies in an examination of, not only the intervention itself, but in an examination of issues with regard to the training qualifications of the interventionists, the timing of the intervention, and the suitability of the intervention for the recipient groups and/or the nature of the adversity (e.g., acute situational adversity versus chronic illness, ongoing psychosocial discord, physical pain, physical scarring, protracted legal difficulties, a long-term rehabilitative process, etc.). Clearly, crisis intervention technologies such as CISD and CISM are best directed toward acute situational adversity, well circumscribed stressors, and acute adult-onset traumatic reactions (Dyregrov, 1997, 1998, 1999; Richards, 1999; Everly & Mitchell, 1999). Thus, the inclusion of crisis intervention in any review of "treatments" for PTSD (Foa, Keane, & Friedman, (2000) seems questionable. Crisis intervention is not a form of therapy per se, nor a substitute for treatment. Crisis intervention, in general, and CISD and CISM, specifically, are designed to compliment more traditional psychotherapeutic services. This is readily apparent if one understands that one of the expressed goals of the CISD is to assess the need for continued care, and that the final component of the muilti-component CISM program is the facilitation of a person in crisis to the next level of care, if appropriate.

Dyregrov (1998) has stated, "In my opinion the debate on debriefing is not only a scientific but also a political debate. It entails power and positions in the therapeutic world. As a technique. . .[debriefings] represented a threat to the psychiatric elite." Certainly, at the very least, the debriefing "controversy" is grounded in the semantics of what actually constitutes a debriefing and the applied role of the debriefing in the overall CISM context. In this, we have been very specific about the nature of the debriefing process (CISD), and the overall crisis intervention process (CISM) for we agree with George Engle that rational discourse is, indeed, grounded upon use of terminology in a consistent manner and the consistent operationalization of that same terminology. Reviewing the available literature, both narrative and empirical, the evidence clearly supports the effectiveness of CISD and CISM.

Recalling the research investigations reviewed in this paper an evolutionary trend clearly emerges which may serve as the best summary of both the lexical as well as substantive issues in the field at this point in time. We shall conclude this paper with a summary of that trend:

1) The term "debriefing" as an unspecified intervention. The early first generation of "debriefing" studies (McFarlane, 1988; Kenardy et al., 1996) could not define the term debriefing, nor could they describe what actually happened, if anything, during the debriefing. Their contribution to our understanding of debriefing is to underscore the need to verify the nature and existence of the intervention.

2) The use of the term "debriefing" to mean individual counseling and individual early intervention with medical patients. The second generation of "debriefing" studies was conducted with medical patients using an individualized intervention format (Bisson et al., 1997; Hobbs et al., 1996; Mayou, Ehlers, & Hobbs, 2000; Lee, Slade, & Lygo, 1996; Small et al., 2000). Their contribution to our understanding of debriefing is that a) crisis intervention is clearly not a substitute for psychotherapy but may be very helpful nevertheless (Small et al., 2000), b) crisis intervention is probably not suitable for patients in acute medical distress in that it is not a substitute for analgesia, physical rehabilitation, psychological rehabilitation, reconstructive surgery, or financial counseling. These studies have also clearly shown that it is premature to reach any adverse conclusions with regard to debriefings (Bisson, McFarlane, & Rose, 2000).

3) The use of the term "debriefing" to mean Critical Incident Stress Debriefing (CISD). The third generation of debriefing studies employed the CISD model of group-format debriefing (Mitchell & Everly, 1997). These studies conducted by Nurmi (1999), Bohl (1991), Chemtob et al. (1997), Wee et al (1999), Jenkins (1996), Everly and Boyle (1999) in a meta-analytic investigation, Deahl, et al. (2000) in a randomized design, and Watchorn (2000) clearly support the assertion that the CISD

model of "debriefing" can be an effective clinical tool for reducing psychological distress, reducing alcohol use, and in preventing PTSD. Their contribution to our understanding of "debriefing" is demonstrating the value of a standardized, theoretically based, empirically developed protocol for small group crisis intervention.

4) Finally, the use of the term "debriefing" to refer to multi-component crisis intervention programs is clearly a misnomer. The term Critical Incident Stress Management (CISM), as defined earlier, is the term indicative of a comprehensive, multi-faceted approach to crisis intervention (Everly & Mitchell, 1999; Flannery, 1998). Studies such as the randomized trial conducted by Bordow & Porritt (1979) and the pre-test post-test open outcome in-patient investigation conducted by Busuttil et al (1995) provided early support for the necessity of a multi-faceted, CISM-like approach. Later studies by Flannery (Flannery, Everly, & Eyler, 2000), Everly (Everly, Flannery, & Eyler, in press), and Richards (1999) have shown repeatedly that the CISM approach to crisis intervention is a clinically effective intervention. The contribution of these studies to our current understanding of the larger field of crisis intervention is the notion that crisis intervention should not consist of a single intervention, but rather, should be an integrated multi-faceted intervention (British Psychological Society, 1990; Mitchell & Everly, 1997; Turnbull, Busuttil, & Pittman, 1997; Richards, 1999; Bordow & Porritt, 1979). As Bisson, McFarlane, & Rose (2000) have stated, one-shot debriefing as a stand-alone crisis intervention cannot be recommended at this time, but there is evidence that debriefing, as part of a multi-faceted crisis intervention, is well received by most people. TABLE 1 offers a prototypic multi-component CISM approach to crisis intervention.

References

Artiss, K. (1963). Human behavior under stress: From combat to social psychiatry. *Military Medicine, 128*, 1011-1015.

Athey, J.L., O'Malley, P., Henderson, D.P., & Ball, J. (1997). Emergency medical services for children: Beyond the lights and sirens. *Professional Psychology: Research and Practice, 28*, 464-470.

Bisson, J.I., McFarlane, A., & Rose, S. (2000). Psychological debriefing. In Foa, E., McFarlance, A., & Friedman, M., (Eds).

Effective Treatments for PTSD (pp. 39-59). NY: Guilford.

Bisson, J.I., Jenkins, P., Alexander, J., & Bannister, C. (1997). Randomized controlled trial of psychological debriefings for victims of acute burn trauma. *British Journal of Psychiatry, 171*, 78-81.

Blampied, N.M. (2000). Single-case research designs: A neglected alternative. *American Psychologist, 55*, 960.

Bohl, N. (1991). The effectiveness of brief psychological

interventions in police officers after critical incidents. In J.T. Reese, J. Horn, and C. Dunning (Eds). *Critical Incidents in Policing, Revised* (pp.31-38). Washington, D.C.: Department of Justice.

Bordow, S. & Porritt, D. (1979). An experimental evaluation of crisis intervention. *Social Science and Medicine, 13*, 251-256.

British Psychological Society (1990). *Psychological Aspects of Disaster.* Leicester: British Psychological Society.

Bunn, T. & Clarke, A. (1979). Crisis intervention. *British Journal of Medical Psychology, 52*, 191-195.

Busuttil, A. & Busuttil, W. (1995) Psychological debriefing. *British Journal of Psychiatry, 166*, 676-677.

Caplan, G. (1961). *An Approach to Community Mental Health. NY:* Grune and Stratton.

Caplan, G. (1964). *Principles of Preventive Psychiatry.* NY: Basic Books.

Campbell, D.T. & Stanley, J.C. (1963). *Experimental and Quasi-experimental Designs for Research.* Chicago: Rand McNally.

Deahl, M., Srinivasan, M., Jones, N., Thomas, J., Neblett, C., & Jolly, A. (2000). Preventing psychological trauma in soldiers: The role of operational stress training and psychological debriefing. *British Journal of Medical Psychology, 73*, 77-85.

Decker, J. & Stubblebine, J (1972). Crisis intervention and prevention of psychiatric disability: A follow-up. *American Journal of Psychiatry, 129*, 725-729.

Dyregrov, A. (1997). The process of psychological debriefing. *Journal of Traumatic Stress, 10*, 589-604.

Dyregrov, A. (1998). Psychological debriefing: An effective method? *TRAUMATOLOGYe, 4 (2),* Article 1.

Dyregrov, A. (1999). Helpful and hurtful aspects of psychological debriefing groups. *International Journal of Emergency Mental Health, 1*, 175-181.

Dyregrov, A. & Mitchell, J. (1992). Work with traumatized children—Psychological effects and coping strategies. *Journal of Traumatic Stress, 5*, 5-17

Everly, G.S., Jr. (1999). Emergency mental health: An overview. *International Journal of Emergency Mental Health, 1*, 3-7.

Everly, G.S., Jr. (2000a). Crisis management briefings (CMB): Large group crisis intervention in response to terrorism, disasters, and violence. *International Journal of Emergency Mental Health, 2*, 53-57.

Everly, G.S., Jr. (2000b). Pastoral crisis intervention: Toward a definition. *International Journal of Emergency Mental Health, 2*, 69-71.

Everly, G.S., Jr. & Boyle, S. (1999). Critical Incident Stress Debriefing (CISD): A meta-analysis. *International Journal of Emergency Mental Health, 1*, 165-168.

Everly, G.S., Jr., Flannery, R.B., Jr., & Eyler, V. (in press). Comprehensive crisis intervention: A statistical review of the literature. *Psychiatric Quarterly,* in press.

Everly, G.S., Jr., Flannery, R.B., & Mitchell, J.T. (2000). Critical Incident Stress Management: A review of literature. *Aggression and Violent Behavior: A Review Journal, 5*, 23-40.

Everly, Jr., G.S. & Mitchell, J.T. (1999). *Critical Incident Stress Management (CISM). A New Era and Standard of Care in Crisis Intervention.* Ellicott City, MD: Chevron.

Figley, C. R. (Ed.). (1995). *Compassion Fatigue: Coping with Secondary Stress Disorder in Those Who Treat the Traumatized.* NY: Brunner/Mazel.

Flannery, R.B., Jr. (1998). *The Assaulted Staff Action Program.* Ellicott City, MD: Chevron.

Flannery, R.B., Jr. (1999a). Treating family survivors of mass casualties: A CISM family crisis intervention approach. *International Journal of Emergency Mental Health, 1* ,243-250.

Flannery, R.B., Jr. (1999b). Critical Incident Stress Management (CISM): The assaultive psychiatric patient. *International Journal of Emergency Mental Health, 1*, 169-174.

Flannery, R.B., Jr. (1999c). Critical Incident Stress Management and the Assaulted Staff Action Program. *International Journal of Emergency Mental Health, 1*, 103-108.

Flannery, R.B., Jr. (in press) Assaulted Staff Action Program (ASAP): Ten years of empirical support for Critical Incident Stress Management (CISM). *International Journal of Emergency Mental Health.*

Flannery, R.B., Jr., Everly, G.S., Jr., & Eyler, V. (2000). The Assaulted Staff Action Program (ASAP) and declines in Assaults: A meta-analysis. *International Journal of Emergency Mental Health, 2*, 143-146.

Flannery, R.B., Jr., Hanson, M., Penk, W., Flannery, G. & Gallagher, C.(1995). The Assaulted Staff Action Program: An approach to coping with the aftermath of violence in the workplace. In L. Murphy, I. Hurrell, S. Sauter, and G. Keita (Eds.). *Job Stress Interventions* (pp. 199-212). Washington, D.C.: APA Press.

Flannery, R.B., Jr., Penk, W., & Corrigan, M. (1999). The Assaulted Staff Action Program (ASAP) and declines in the prevalence of assaults: A community-based replication. *International Journal of Emergency Mental Health, 1*, 19-22.

Flannery, R.B., Jr., Anderson, E., Marks, L., & Uzoma, L. (2000). The Assaulted Staff Action Program (ASAP) and declines in rates of assaults: Mixed replicated findings. *Psychiatric Quarterly, 71,* 165-175.

Flannery, R.B., Jr., Hanson, M., Penk, W., Goldfinger, S., Pastva, G., & Navon, M. (1998). *Psychiatric Services, 49,* 241-243.

Foa, E., Keane, T., & Friedman, M. (2000). *Effective Treatments for PTSD.* NY: Guilford.

Hersen, M. & Barlow, D. (1976). *Single-case Experimental Designs:* Oxford, England: Pergamon.

Hobbs, M., Mayou, R., Harrison, B. & Worlock, P. (1996). A randomized controlled trial of psychological debriefing for victims of road traffic accidents. *British Medical Journal, 313*, 1438-1439.

Jenkins, S.R. (1996). Social support and debriefing efficacy among emergency medical workers after a mass shooting incident. *Journal of Social Behavior and Personality, 11*, 477 - 492.

Kenardy, J.A. (2000). The current status of psychological debriefing. *British Medical Journal, 321*, 1032-1033.

Kenardy, J.A., Webster, R.A., Lewin, T.J., Carr, V.J., Hazell, P.L., & Carter, G.L. (1996). Stress debriefing and patterns of recovery following a natural disaster. *Journal of Traumatic Stress, 9*, 37 - 49.

Kraus, R.P. (1997). Randomised controlled trial of psychological debriefing for victims of acute burn trauma: Comment. *British Journal of psychiatry, 171*, 583.

Langsley, D., Machotka, P., & Flomenhaft, K. (1971). Avoiding mental health admission: A follow-up. *American Journal of Psychiatry, 127*, 1391-1394.

Lee, C., Slade, P., & Lygo, V. (1996). The influence of psychological debriefing on emotional adaptation in women following early miscarriage. *British Journal of Psychiatry, 69*, 47-58.

Mayou, R.A., Ehlers, A., & Hobbs, M. (2000). Psychological debriefing for road traffic accident victims: Three-year follow-up of a randomised controlled trial. *British Journal of Psychiatry, 176*, 589-593.

McFarlane, A.C. (1988). The longitudinal course of posttraumatic morbidity. *Journal of Nervous and Mental Disease, 176*, 30 - 39.

Miller, L. (1999). Critical incident stress debriefing: Clinical applications and new directions. *International Journal of Emergency Mental Health, 1*, 253-265.

Mitchell, J.T. (1983). When disaster strikes...The critical incident stress debriefing process. *Journal of Emergency*

Medical Services, 8, (1), 36-39.

Mitchell, J.T. & Everly, G.S., Jr. (1997). Critical Incident Stress Debriefing: An Operations Manual for the Prevention of Traumatic Stress Among Emergency Services and Disaster Workers (2nd Edition). Ellicott City, MD: Chevron.

Mitchell, J.T., Schiller, G., Eyler, V., & Everly, G.S. (1999). Community crisis intervention: The Coldenham tragedy revisited. International Journal of Emergency Mental Health, 1, 227-238.

Newman, E.C. (2000). Group crisis intervention in a school setting following an attempted suicide. International Journal of Emergency Mental Health, 2, 97-100.

Nurmi, L. (1999). The sinking of the Estonia: The effects of Critical Incident Stess Debriefing on Rescuers. International Journal of Emergency Mental Health, 1, 23-32.

OSHA. (1996). Guidelines for Preventing Workplace Violence for Health Care and Social Service Workers - OSHA 3148-1996. Washington, D.C.: Author.

OSHA. (1998). Recommendations for Workplace Violence Prevention Programs in Late-Night Retail Establishments. - OSHA 3153-1998. Washington, D.C.: Author.

Parad, L. & Parad, H. (1968). A study of crisis oriented planned short-term treatment: Part II. Social Casework, 49, 418-426.

Richards, D. (1999, April) A field study of CISD vs. CISM. Paper presented to the 5th World Congress on Stress, Trauma, and Coping, Baltimore.

Robinson, R.C. & Mitchell, J.T. (1993). Evaluation of psychological debriefings. Journal of Traumatic Stress, 6(3), 367 - 382.

Robinson, R.C. & Mitchell, J.T. (1995). Getting Some Balance Back into the Debriefing Debate. The Bulletin of the Australian Psychological Society, 17 (10), 5 - 10.

Rose, S. & Bisson, J. (1998). Brief early psychological interventions following trauma: A systematic review of literature. Journal of Traumatic Stress, 11, 697-710.

Seligman, M.E.P. (1995). The effectiveness of psychotherapy. American Psychologist, 109, 993-994.

Shannon, P.A. (1991). The crisis of the caregivers. Critical Care Nursing Clinics of North America, 3, 353-359.

Small, R., Lumley, J., Donohue, L., Potter, A., & Waldenstrom, U. (2000). Randomised controlled trial of midwife led debriefing to reduce maternal depression after operative childbirth. British Medical Journal, 321, 1043-1047.

Solomon, Z. & Benbenishty, R. (1986). The role of proximity, immediacy, and expectancy in frontline treatment of combat stress reaction among Israelis in the Lebanon War. American Journal of Psychiatry, 143, 613-617.

Swanson, W.C., & Carbon, J.B. (1989). Crisis intervention: Theory and Technique. In Task Force Report of the American Psychiatric Association. Treatments of Psychiatric Disorders. Wash. D.C.: APA Press.

Turnbull, G., Busuttil, W., & Pittman, S. (1997). Psychological debriefing for victims of acute burn trauma. British Journal of Psychiatry, 171, 582.

Watchorn, J.(2000, August). Role of debriefing in the prevention of PTSD. Paper presented to the Inaugural Conference on Stress, Trauma, & Coping in the Emergency services and Allied Professions. Melbourne, Australia.

Wee, D.F., Mills, D.M. & Koelher, G. (1999). The effects of Critical Incident Stress Debriefing on emergency medical services personnel following the Los Angeles civil disturbance. International Journal of Emergency Mental Health, 1, 33-38.

Wessley, S., Rose, S., & Bisson, J. (1998). A systematic review of brief psychological interventions (debriefing) for the treatment of immediate trauma related symptoms and the prevention of post traumatic stress disorder (C o c h r a n e

Review). *Cochrane Library,* Issue 3, Oxford, UK: Update Software.

Western Management Consultants. (1996). *The*

Medical Services Branch CISM Evaluation Report. Vancouver, B.C.: Author.

Yalom, I. (1970). *Group Psychotherapy.* NY: Basic.

DEBRIEFINGS (PD)

"Since PD is fully accepted as standard
practice for emergency services
personnel and well-received by group
members and organizations, it is hard
to find fault in its application in a mass
disaster such as the terrorist attacks…
on September 11, 2001."
(Litz, et al., Clin. Psyc. 2002)

Findings more recent and more
relevant to disaster mental
health tend to support the use
of crisis intervention…

LESSONS LEARNED FROM
CONSULTATION MENTAL HEALTH-
EXPANDING COCHRANE
(Stapleton, Medical Crisis Intervention, 2004)

- 11 (10/11 RCT) studies of individual crisis
  intervention in medical settings
- 16 outcomes
- 2124 subjects
- Overall effectiveness: Cohen's d = .44
  (anxiety, .52; depression, .24; PTS, .57)

LESSONS LEARNED FROM CONSULTATION MENTAL HEALTH
(Stapleton, Medical Crisis Intervention, 2004)

ᴥ Early Psychological Intervention is improved by increased training (Cohen's d = .57 vs. .29)

ᴥ Early Psychological Intervention outcome is enhanced via multiple sessions (.60 vs .33) (plateau at 2-3 sessions, Boscarino, et al., 2005)

LESSONS LEARNED FROM CONSULTATION MENTAL HEALTH
(Stapleton, Medical Crisis Intervention, 2004)

ᴥ Early Psychological Intervention is enhanced via the use of multiple interventions on PTS (.62 vs .55)

LESSONS LEARNED FROM THE WORKPLACE

Post disaster crisis intervention (CISM) was associated with reduced risk for

- binge drinking (d=.74),

- alcohol dependence (.92),

- PTSD symptoms (.56),

- major depression (.81),

LESSONS LEARNED FROM THE WORKPLACE

Post disaster crisis intervention (CISM) was associated with reduced risk for

- anxiety disorder (.98), , and

- global impairment (.66),

- compared with comparable individuals who did not receive this intervention (Boscarino, et al, IJEMH, 2005).

"There is now emerging evidence that prompt delivery of brief, acute phase services in the first weeks after an event can lead to sustained reduction in morbidity years later, reducing the burden of secondary functional impairment, presumed daily average life years lost (DALYS), and costs to both the individual and the public" (p.15).

Schreiber, M. (Summer, 2005). PsySTART rapid mental health triage and incident command system. The Dialogue: A Quarterly Technical assistance Bulletin on Disaster Behavioral health, 14-15.

Value added of Crisis Intervention: Screening & Increasing Access to Care

- Only 11% of victims of violent crime responded to institutional invitations to express attitudes regarding crime & punishment (Rose, et al., Psychological Medicine, 1999).

- Formal mental health utilization post 9/11 increased only ~ 3% in civilians and emergency personnel even though prevalence of PTSD estimated at 7 -20% and depression at ~9% (see JHCPHP, 2005)

Value added of Crisis Intervention:
Screening & Increasing Access to Care

ﻼ Clients who were told about the crisis intervention
approach were less likely to withdraw from
intervention programs against MH advice
compared to those not given short-term
expectations
(Parad & Parad, Social Casework, 1968).

ﻼ First responders, military personnel, and
civilian disaster workers (North, et al., 2002, J. T.
Stress; Hoge et al. 2004, NEJM; Jayasinghe, et al.,
2005, IJEMH) often resistant to seeking MH
treatment, therefore crisis intervention may be
their only access to mental health services

ﻼ Up to 76% of those that go on to develop
posttraumatic morbidity may show predictors
within 24 hours (North, et al., 1999, JAMA)

ﻼ EARLY PSYCHOLOGICAL
INTERVENTION SHOULD NOT BE USED
SPECIFICALLY AS A MEANS TO
PREVENT PTSD; RATHER, consider as a
platform for screening, reducing acute distress,
fostering group cohesion, providing info,
anticipatory guidance (Litz, et al., 2002, Clin
Psychol; Everly & Langlieb, 2003, IJEMH; Arendt &
Elklit, 2001, Acta Psyc Scand)

From Tactical to Strategic...

➣ Critical Incident Stress Management (CISM) found to be effective in reducing distress in response to robberies (Richards, JMentHlth, 2001) and in reducing assaults and related distress upon healthcare staff (Flannery, 1999, ASAP; IJEMH, 2001)

➣ 10 year analysis of ASAP CISM reveals method to be consistently effective (Flannery, IJEMH, 2001)

OTHER REVIEWS...

LAW ENFORCEMENT SURVEY- 2003 (Sheehan, et al., FBI LEB, 2004)

➣ Review of selected Federal law enforcement and other key law enforcement agencies practices:

➣ Recognition of the value of early psychological intervention/ critical incident response.

➣ The utilization of a phase-sensitive, multi-component crisis intervention system as part of an overall continuum of care was employed/ recommended by all organizations sampled.

LAW ENFORCEMENT SURVEY- 2003
(Sheehan, et al., FBI LEB, 2004)

- Tactical interventions, in most programs, included the ability to perform 1:1 crisis intervention, small group crisis intervention, large group crisis intervention, family support services, as well as the ability to access spiritual support services and treatment services.

EMPLOYEE ASSISTANCE PROFESSIONAL'S ASSN – DISASTER RESPONSE TASK FORCE (EAPA, 2002)

- EAPs should develop workplace disaster plans.
- Plans should consist of a continuum of interventions:
  - Pre-Incident Training / Coordination (early intervention CISM training, resiliency training, risk assessment, policy development)
  - Acute Response
  - Post-Incident Response (defusing, CISD, crisis management briefings, assessment/ referral, self-care)
  - Follow-up (supervisory briefings, assessment, training)
  - Post-Incident review and plan reformulation

REASONABLE EVIDENCE-BASED CONCLUSIONS

- More, better controlled, research needed

- Care must be taken

- Data reviewed support use of group "debriefing" with emergency services personnel (Arendt & Elklit, 2001)

- Data reviewed tend to support use of group "debriefing" subsequent to disasters, war, robbery (see NIMH, 2002, tables 2-3;)

REASONABLE EVIDENCE-BASED CONCLUSIONS

- Data do not support single session individualized interventions after medical, surgical distress with minimal training

- Data support multi-component intervention systems

- NIMH (2002), Institute of Medicine (2003) recommend acute phase "psychological first aid" (no direct data available)

CRISIS INTERVENTION (CI): KEY POINTS

- Crisis intervention (CI) has a rich history having been developed along two evolutionary pathways:
  1) community mental health and suicide intervention, and
  2) military psychiatry.
- Crisis intervention is not a form of psychotherapy, nor a substitute for psychotherapy.
- As physical first aid is to surgery, crisis intervention is to psychotherapy

---

- As described herein, crisis intervention is not intended to be the practice of psychiatry, psychology, social work, nor counseling, per se, it is simply psychological/emotional first aid

- As described herein, consistent with NIMH guidelines and Federal "crisis counseling" models, crisis intervention may be practiced by mental health clinicians, as well as, medical personnel, clergy, & community volunteers (although we believe mental health guidance, supervision, or oversight is essential)

IN 1990, THE BRITISH PSYCHOLOGICAL SOCIETY RECOMMENDED THAT CRISIS INTERVENTION SHOULD BE MULTI-COMPONENT IN NATURE.

➢Raphael (1986) was the first to write most eloquently on the need to view crisis intervention services reaching across a continuum.

➢A review of key documents reveals a vast array of potential interventions that may be employed...

Recent recommendations for early intervention include the use of a variety of interventions matched to the needs of the situation and the recipient populations

(Mental Health & Mass Violence, 2002; IOM, 2003)

The Johns Hopkins'
RESISTANCE, RESILIENCE, RECOVERY
An outcome-driven continuum of care

Create Resistance   Enhance Resiliency   Speed Recovery

Assessment   Assessment   Assessment
Intervention   Intervention   Intervention
Evaluation   Evaluation   Evaluation

[Kaminsky, et al, (2005) RESISTANCE, RESILIENCE, RECOVERY. In Everly & Parker,
Mental Health Aspects of Disaster: Public Health Preparedness and Response. Balto: Johns
Hopkins Center for Public Health Preparedness.

In the present context, the term *resistance* refers to the ability of an individual, a group, an organization, or even an entire population, to literally **resist** manifestations of clinical distress, impairment, or dysfunction associated with critical incidents, terrorism, and even mass disasters.

Resistance may be thought of as a form of psychological / behavioral *immunity* to distress and dysfunction.

Resistance may be best built via pre-incident / pre-deployment training.

In the present context, the term *resilience* refers to the ability of an individual, a group, an organization, or even an entire population, to **rapidly and effectively rebound** from psychological and / or behavioral perturbations associated with critical incidents, terrorism, and even mass disasters.

It is likely that early psychological intervention (i.e., response oriented crisis and disaster mental health intervention) is best thought of as a means of enhancing resiliency.

The term *recovery* refers to the ability of an individual, a group, an organization, or even an entire population, to literally **recover the ability to adaptively function,** both psychologically and behaviorally, in the wake of a significant clinical distress, impairment, or dysfunction subsequent to critical incidents, terrorism, and even mass disasters.

Treatment and rehabilitation programs are most likely the interventions of choice to speed recovery.

Categories of Disaster Mental Health Interventions
(adapted from NVOAD- EPI Subcommittee Consensus Points, 2005)

- Pre-incident training
- Incident assessment and strategic planning
- Risk and crisis communication
- Acute psychological assessment and triage
- Crisis intervention with large groups

Categories of Disaster Mental Health Interventions
(adapted from NVOAD- EPI Subcommittee Consensus Points, 2005)

- Crisis intervention with small groups
- Crisis intervention with individuals, face-to-face and hotlines
- Crisis planning and intervention with communities
- Crisis planning and intervention with organizations
- Psychological first aid

Categories of Disaster Mental Health Interventions
(adapted from NVOAD- EPI Subcommittee Consensus Points, 2005)

- Facilitating access to appropriate levels of care when needed
- Assisting special and diverse populations
- Spiritual assessment and care
- Self care and family care including safety and security
- Post incident evaluation and training based on lessons learned

One approach, that has been frequently used, to integrate such an array of crisis / disaster mental health interventions across a continuum of need is **Critical Incident Stress Management** (CISM; Everly & Mitchell, 1999).

CRITICAL INCIDENT STRESS MANAGEMENT (CISM)
(Everly & Mitchell, 1997, 1999; Everly & Langlieb, 2003)

A comprehensive, phase sensitive, and integrated,

multi-component approach to crisis/disaster intervention.

CISM is a strategic intervention system.

It possesses numerous tactical interventions.

A Comprehensive, Integrated Multi-Component
Crisis Intervention System
(adapted from: Martha Starr)

Each "leaf"
represents a
specific tactical
intervention.

ELEMENTS OF CISM

➤ Pre-incident education, preparation

➤ Assessment

➤ Strategic Planning

➤ Large Group Crisis Intervention:
- Demobilizations (large groups of rescue / recovery)
- Respite / Rehab Sectors
- Crisis Management Briefings (CMB)

ELEMENTS OF CISM

➤ Small Group Crisis Intervention:
- Defusings (small groups)
- Small group CMB
- "Debriefing" Models: Critical Incident Stress Debriefing (CISD); HERD; NOVA; Multi-stressor debriefing model; CED

ELEMENTS OF CISM

- One-on-one crisis intervention, including individual PFA
- Family CISM
- Organizational / Community intervention, consultation
- Pastoral crisis intervention
- Follow-up and referral for continued care

CORE COMPETENCIES OF COMPREHENSIVE CRISIS INTERVENTION

- Assessment/ triage benign vs. malignant symptoms

- Strategic planning and utilizing an integrated multi-component crisis intervention system within an incident command system

CORE COMPETENCIES OF COMPREHENSIVE CRISIS INTERVENTION

- One-on-one crisis intervention

- Small group crisis intervention

- Large group crisis intervention

- Follow-up and referral

REVIEW:

"The Evolving Nature of Disaster
Mental Health Services"

APPENDIX A provides a brief
overview of numerous crisis.
Disaster mental health interventions.

Figure 1 shows how CISM services may be allocated across the crisis spectrum.

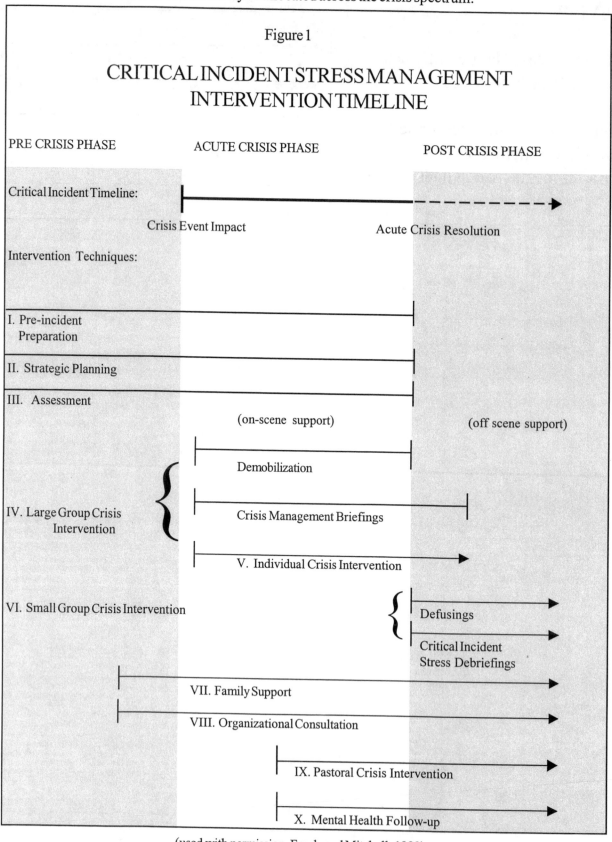

Figure 1

CRITICAL INCIDENT STRESS MANAGEMENT
INTERVENTION TIMELINE

PRE CRISIS PHASE   ACUTE CRISIS PHASE   POST CRISIS PHASE

Critical Incident Timeline:

Crisis Event Impact   Acute Crisis Resolution

Intervention Techniques:

I. Pre-incident
   Preparation

II. Strategic Planning

III. Assessment

(on-scene support)   (off scene support)

Demobilization

IV. Large Group Crisis
    Intervention   Crisis Management Briefings

V. Individual Crisis Intervention

VI. Small Group Crisis Intervention   Defusings

                                             Critical Incident
                                             Stress Debriefings

VII. Family Support

VIII. Organizational Consultation

IX. Pastoral Crisis Intervention

X. Mental Health Follow-up

(used with permission, Everly and Mitchell, 1999)

54

"In all the controversy, criticism and research debate on the merits of debriefing [early intervention], certain constants are emerging. The most effective methods for mitigating the effects of exposure to trauma…, those which will help keep our people healthy and in service, are those which use early intervention, are multi-modal and multi-component. That is, they use different 'active ingredients' …, and these components are used at the appropriate time with the right target group."

Dr Hayden Duggan
International Association of Fire Chiefs' ICHIEFS on-line resource, Sept 1, 2002

The challenge in crisis intervention is not only developing TACTICAL skills in the "core intervention competencies," but is in knowing WHEN
to best STRATEGICALLY employ the most appropriate
intervention for the situation.

STRATEGIC PLANNING FORMULA

1. **THREAT**
2. **TARGET** (Who should receive services? ID target groups.)
3. **TYPE** (What interventions should be used?)
4. **TIMING** (When should the interventions be implemented, with what target groups?)

STRATEGIC PLANNING FORMULA

5. **RESOURCES** (What intervention resources are available to be mobilized for what target groups, when? Consider internal and external resources.)

   [Note: **THEMES** which may modify impact and response should be considered (children, chem-bio hazards, etc?)]

6. Teams - what are our resources, specialities. Will we need to call others?

PEER SUPPORT:
A Special Kind of Crisis Intervention

The provision of crisis intervention services by those other than mental health clinicians and directed toward individuals of similar key characteristics as those of the providers, e.g., emergency services peer support, student peer support, etc.

Jerome Frank, PhD, MD once noted that at the core of psychological healing resides an "anti-demoralization effect"

And,
the ability to engender this effect
in others is often based upon
one's abilities of interpersonal
"influence"
(persuasion)

(Frank. Persuasion & Healing, 1961)

"Ethos," i.e. credibility, is one of
the 3 core elements of
interpersonal influence-
Aristotle

(ethos, pathos, logos)

Peer support personnel have an
"ethos" (credibility) that no
academic training program can
create!

USE PEERS WHEN:

 ❧ Recipient group is specially trained/ educated.

 ❧ Group possesses a unique culture.

 ❧ Group members perceive themselves as unique, little understood, misunderstood.

USE PEERS WHEN:

 ❧ Group extends minimal trust to those outside the group.

 ❧ Generally not necessary with groups from general populations of primary victims.

EMPIRICAL EFFECTIVENESS OF PEERS DOCUMENTED:

Truax & Carkhuff, 1967,
 Toward Effective Counseling
Durlak, 1979,
 Psychological Bulletin
Hattie, Sharpley, Rogers, 1984,
 Psychological Bulletin

CAUTIONS: Peer Support

THE NEED TO WORK WITH PROFESSIONAL
MENTAL HEALTH GUIDANCE / SUPPORT

THE NEED TO VIEW PEER SUPPORT / FIRST AID
AS ONLY ONE POINT ON THE OVERALL
CONTINUUM OF CARE

CAUTIONS: Peer Support

KNOWING WHEN ONE IS OVER ONE'S HEAD
(UNDERESTIMATING SEVERITY)

COUNTERTRANSFERENCE (GETTING TOO
CLOSE; TAKING TOO MUCH FOR GRANTED)

REVIEW:

"Thoughts on Peer
(Paraprofessional) Support"

NOTES

ARE YOU LISTENING?

Section II

GROUP EXERCISE

GROUP EXERCISE

George
Ralph
Dawn
Capt
Tom

HAVING COMPLETED THE GROUP EXERCISE

➤ What role did "ASSUMPTIONS" play?

➤ What role did VALUES play?

➤ What are the implications for COUNTERTRANSFERENCE REACTIONS, especially with regard to PEER INTERVENTIONISTS?

NOTES

CRISIS COMMUNICATION TECHNIQUES

Section III

CRISIS COMMUNICATION
TECHNIQUES

- Paracommunications: Silence and
  Nonverbal Behavior
- "Mirror" Techniques
- Questions
- Action Directives

BEWARE!

Excessive use of silence in crisis
situations can communicate lack of
interest, thus causing an escalation.

Nonverbal behavior sends a
powerful message.
Often, the first impression you make
is based upon how you look.
The challenge is how to make that
impression useful in the service
of crisis intervention.

"MIRROR TECHNIQUES"

- Restatement

- Paraphrase (Summary & Extrapolation)

- Reflection of Emotion (Commonly Used By Hostage Negotiators)

"MIRROR" TECHNIQUES

- Are effective when placed at a natural pause in the conversation

- Or, may be used to redirect the flow of a tangential conversation

- Or, can be used break an escalating emotional spiral

RESTATEMENT

- Takes the other person's words and restates only the term or phrase about which you wish to inquire or emphasize

- Do not overdo this technique

- Demonstrates concern, listening

SUMMARY PARAPHRASE

- Simply summarizes in your words, the main points made by the person in crisis
- Usually inserted when the person pauses
- Stems might include: "So, in other words…" or "Sounds like…" or "What I'm hearing you say is…"

EXTRAPOLATION PARAPHRASE

- People in crisis seldom understand the consequences of their actions
- Extrapolation = summary + consequences
- May be a behavior change tool

REFLECTING EMOTION

- Based upon verbal or nonverbal cues
- Attempts to accurately label the experienced emotion of the other person ("you seem really angry…")
- Builds empathy, rapport
- Encourages ventilation
- Helps defuse anger

COMMUNICATION
EXERCISE:

INTERVIEW USING
SUMMARY PARAPHRASING
&
REFLECTING EMOTION

(Observer's Form #1)

_____

_____

_____

_____

_____

_____

_____

Table 1
BASIC COMMUNICATION TECHNIQUES

TECHNIQUE	PURPOSE	COMMENT
SILENCE	- to promote speech - to encourage continued uninterrupted speech	Careful! May inadvertently communicate noncaring, lack of interest.
NON VERBAL ATTENDING	- to encourage continued uninterrupted speech - to probe - to show interest	Nodding of the head and facial expressions are examples.
RESTATEMENT	- to show you are listening - to check for accuracy - to clarify semantics - to probe	Careful! Used too frequently, you can sound like a mindless parrot. Good to clarify semantic ambiguities.
PARAPHRASING	- to communicate interest, understanding, empathy - to check for listening accuracy to allow speaker to 'hear' own thoughts - to probe for further content	Use more frequently than restatement. Easier and more natural than restatement. A powerful behavior change technique.

REFLECTION OF EMOTION	- to identify the speaker's feelings based on verbal and/or nonverbal cues. - to encourage discussion of feelings and remove emotional blocks to communication	Important to allow feelings to be expressed, otherwise they block problem solving and tend to escalate. But be careful! Don't overuse this technique.
OPEN-END QUESTIONS	- to provide maximal response options - to question without restricting answers.	Good to use in early phases. Use when you get "stuck."
CLOSED-END QUESTIONS	- to direct or focus responses - to provide structure	Good when pursuing a specific target. You only learn what you know to ask.

PARAPHRASING: A SPECIAL TECHNIQUE

Of all of the "mirror techniques," paraphrasing is by far the most useful. Its value is derived from its wide range of utilities. Paraphrasing can be used to:

1. show attentiveness
2. solicit further comment or elaboration
3. demonstrate acceptance or validation
4. foster introspection
5. slow down or interrupt an emotional tirade
6. provide closure to individual or group exchanges
7. alter attitudes, and
8. change behavior.

The decision to change one's behavior ultimately comes from within. Paraphrasing represents a unique opportunity to allow an individual to consider other perspectives or behavioral options not originally considered. Such a technique is often superior in behavior change utility compared to declarative or confrontational statements.

There exist two basic types of paraphrasing:

1. the summary paraphrase, and
2. the extrapolation paraphrase.

In the <u>summary paraphrase</u>, the crisis worker merely summarizes, in his / her own words, the key comments of the person in crisis.

In the <u>extrapolation paraphrase</u>, the crisis worker takes the comments of the person in crisis and extends them to a logical result or conclusion.

PERSON IN CRISIS: "My life is horrible. I've lost my job and I worry about being able to support my family. They really depend on me. I feel so depressed that I sometimes consider ending it all."

SUMMARY #1:   "You sound overwhelmed with life right now."

SUMMARY #2:   "It sounds like you're feeling so overwhelmed that you've even considered suicide."

EXTRAPOLATION #1: "So, in other words, you're so overwhelmed with life right now that you've even considered suicide; regardless of how it would affect your family and friends."

EXTRAPOLATION #2: "So things have gotten so bad that you've considered suicide, even though your death will have a devastating effect on your family and friends."

The summary paraphrase can prove very useful in group crisis interventions such as defusings and debriefings, while the extrapolation paraphrase should be avoided therein.

Clearly, the extrapolation paraphrase may possess an implied behavior change component.

The use of the extrapolation paraphrase should not be confused with the complex psychotherapeutic technique known as <u>interpretation</u>.

Interpretation entails having the crisis worker attempt to identify the meaning or motive undergirding the behavior of the person in crisis.

Interpretation: "It seems to me that the reason you're considering suicide is that its a way of avoiding the embarrassment, or guilt, associated with bankruptcy."

Interpretation should usually be avoided by the crisis worker in that it may take considerable time and effort for the person in crisis to come to understand the interpretation, especially if it taps unconscious motives.

SUMMARY PARAPHRASING
Exercise

DIRECTIONS:
Listed below are 4 statements. Write an appropriate <u>summary</u> <u>paraphrase</u> for each.

1. "I'm so angry, I just don't know what to do."

2. "I'm so overwhelmed by life that I've considered killing myself."

3. "In this organization, we have a set body of rules and regulations that we must adhere to regardless of the circumstances, with no exceptions."

4. "If I don't like someone, I just tell them so. I think its better to just be upfront and honest, no matter what."

EXTRAPOLATION PARAPHRASING
Exercise

DIRECTIONS:
Listed below are 4 statements. Write an appropriate extrapolation paraphrase for each.

1. "I'm so angry, I just don't know what to do."

2. "I'm so overwhelmed by life that I've considered killing myself."

3. "In this organization, we have a set body of rules and regulations that we must adhere to regardless of the circumstances, with no exceptions."

4. "If I don't like someone, I just tell them so. I think its better to just be upfront and honest, no matter what."

So you value honesty above other personal qualities
Have you ever considered the consequences of being brutally honest with an individual whose mental health is fragile?

OBSERVER'S FEEDBACK FORM
#1
<u>Active Listening Exercise</u>

1. Use of silence:

2. Body language / posture conducive to communication:

3. Appropriate choice of verbal language:

4. Use of restatement:

5. Use of emotional reflection:

6. Use of paraphrasing:
   a. Summary:

   b. Extrapolation:

7. Was the exchange conversational? Did it have a natural flow?

8. Overall, what improvements could be made?

QUESTIONS AND THE "DIAMOND" COMMUNICATION STRUCTURE

Section
IV

QUESTIONS

☞ CLOSED-END ("do you...?" "Is this...?" "Did you...?")

☞ Multiple choice

☞ Open-end ("How?" "What")

☞ Remember, paraphrases and reflections are closed-end questions

A simple structure for asking questions is called the "diamond" structure.

QUESTIONS

Questions fall on a continuum which is bounded by the functional concepts of directive and nondirective at the bipolar extremes.

Directive questions are questions which serve to constrain or restrict the response options available to the respondent. The most directive question is the closed-end question known as the "yes – no" question. Multiple choice questions are also variations of the closed-end directive question.

"Is this the car that was involved in the accident?" (yes – no)
"Was the car involved in the accident a Ford or a Chevy?" (multiple choice)

The advantages of the directive questions are that they are efficient and focused interrogatories. The disadvantage is that they are weak in their ability to generate unanticipated information.

Nondirective questions are questions which serve by not restricting the response options available to the respondent. Open-end questions are a form of nondirective question.

"What type of car was involved in the accident?" (open-end)

Although not always efficient, the open-end question is a powerful mechanism by which the crisis worker can generate a great deal of information about any given topic, assuming the other individual is, indeed, willing to communicate.

"Tell me, what happened here?" is another example of the open-end question.

ACTION DIRECTIVES

Action directives are statements suggesting that a specific type of action, or problem-solving plan, should be initiated. Any form of encouragement would also fit under the category.

If a crisis worker suggests that a particular action be taken by the person in crisis, it is important to understand that the crisis worker now "owns" some of the responsibility for such a suggestion and its ultimate outcome.

"DIAMOND" STRUCTURE

- ✒ Begin asking closed-ended questions in order to establish basic facts
- ✒ Move to open-ended questions in order to probe and obtain more information
- ✒ Use paraphrase and reflection of emotion to summarize key points and acknowledge emotions

CLOSED END QUESTION ("YES-NO")
TO ESTABLISH FACTS

OPEN QUESTIONS
TO PROBE/ EXPAND

PARAPHRASE (closed question)
TO SUMMARIZE

ACTION DIRECTIVES

- ✒ Providing direction on what to do

- ✒ If someone asks a direct question, it is usually best to provide a direct answer, unless the answer will cause an escalation of the crisis

COMMUNICATION EXERCISE:

EMPHASIZING USE OF
YES-NO QUESTIONS
(Be sure to use open-end questions,
paraphrasing & reflection of
emotion)

(Use Observer's Form #2)

_____

_____

_____

_____

_____

_____

_____

OPEN vs. CLOSED-ENDED QUESTIONS

Exercise

DIRECTIONS:

Take the following closed-ended questions and convert them to open-ended questions.

1. Is your favorite color red?

2. Were you depressed when your mother died?

3. What medication should be prescribed, Valium?

4. How did you feel when you were told you were fired, were you angry?

OBSERVER'S FEEDBACK FORM
#2
Integrative Listening Exercise

1. Use of silence:

2. Body language / posture conducive to communication:

3. Appropriate choice of verbal language:

4. Use of restatement:

5. Use of emotional reflection:

6. Use of paraphrasing:
   a. Summary:

b. Extrapolation:

7. Use of open-end questions:

8. Use of closed-end questions:

9. Was the exchange conversational? Did it have a natural flow?

10. Overall, what improvements could be made?

NOTES

PSYCHOLOGICAL REACTIONS IN CRISIS

Section
V

EUSTRESS vs. DISTRTESS vs. DYSFUNCTION

Three intensity levels of stress:

Eustress = Positive, motivating stress

Distress = Excessive stress

Dysfunction = Impairment

THE SEA−3 MENTAL STATUS EXAM

The mental status examination typically attempts to assess the person's mental state by observing the person's appearance (dress and grooming) and behavior (posture, facial expressions, body movements, amplitude and quality of speech, and helper−helpee interactions). The crisis worker usually asks questions about the person's feelings, thoughts and perceptions (intellectual functioning, orientation, insight, judgement, memory, thought content and stream of thought). Remembering all of those evaluation criteria can be a challenge, especially in a crisis. The SEA-3 method of mental status examination provides an easy to remember outline to aid the crisis worker in evaluating the distressed individual.

SPEECH

amplitude, quality
flow, organization

EMOTION

dominant mood
appropriateness
absence, euphoria, depressed
anger, hostility, fear, anxiety, apprehension

APPEARANCE

unkempt, unclean
clothing disheveled, dirty, atypical, unusual, bizarre
unusual physical characteristics

ALERTNESS

oriented to person, place and time
insight, judgement
memory, intellectual functioning
stream, content of thought

ACTIVITY

facial expressions
posture
movements
interactions with helper

PSYCHOLOGICAL REACTIONS TO CRISIS AND TRAUMA

ABREACTION: an acute emotional discharge or tirade that has cathartic characteristics.

ACUTE PSYCHOGENIC COGNITIVE IMPAIRMENT: a transitory episode of cognitive impairment initiated by extreme stress. Symptoms may include attention deficit, dyscalculia, anomia, etc. (See cortical inhibition syndrome).

BRIEF PSYCHOTIC REACTION: an acute reactionary loss of reality contact characterized by hallucinations and / or delusions.

BURNOUT: a condition of psychological exhaustion wherein mental health has <u>eroded</u> over time due to chronic exposure to nontraumatic stressors.

DISSOCIATION: an acute state of depersonalization and / or derealization. Peritraumatic dissociation may be an excellent predictor of subsequent trauma morbidity.

MAJOR DEPRESSION: a condition of depressed mood combined with appetite disturbance, reduced libido, sleep disturbance, lethargy and / or psychomotor retardation. Self perceptions of hopelessness and / or helplessness may also be in evidence (See Figure 2).

Figure 2
BASIC PSYCHOLOGICAL PROCESSES AND THEIR EXTREMES

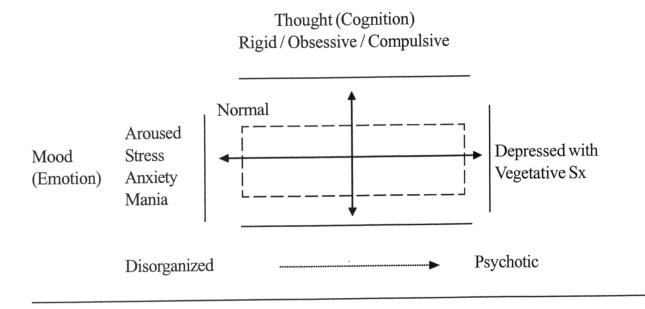

PANIC DISORDER: an acute episode of extreme stress, often including tachycardia, sweating, a feeling of suffocation, hyperventilation and other symptoms of sympathetic or parasympathetic nervous system over arousal. See Figure 2.

PATHOLOGICAL GRIEF: a bereavement reaction that is excessive (debilitating intensity and / or chronicity) may be evidenced by extreme guilt, psychomotor retardation, negative affect, depression, feelings of worthlessness.

POSTTRAUMATIC STRESS (PTS): a normal, predictable psychological reaction to a traumatic event. Such a reaction is often characterized by recollections of the trauma, sleep disturbance, hyperstartle reactions, hypervigilence and avoidance behaviors. This constellation of symptoms is thought to have survival value if acute and non-generalizable.

POSTTRAUMATIC STRESS DISORDER (PTSD): a pathognomonic variation of posttraumatic stress. It is characterized by 3 symptom clusters: intrusive memories of the event, stress arousal symptoms, numbing, and avoidance reactions. Symptoms must persist for a minimum of 30 days and must cause significant distress and / or dysfunction. Psychosomatic symptoms may develop as a result of PTSD. A model of PTSD is offered in Figures 3 and 4.

PSYCHOSOMATIC DISORDER: an organically-based manifestation of physical (medical) symptoms. A physical illness initiated, or worsened, by psychological processes. A psychophysiological disorder.

SOMATOFORM DISORDER: a psychologically-based dysfunction within the sensory or motor systems, without known organic pathogenesis.

STRESS: a psychophysiological response to a stressor; "wear and tear;" the aging process; the "fight or flight" response (See Everly, 1989).

Figure 3

POSTTRAUMATIC STRESS DISORDER (PTSD)
(Everly and Lating, 1995)

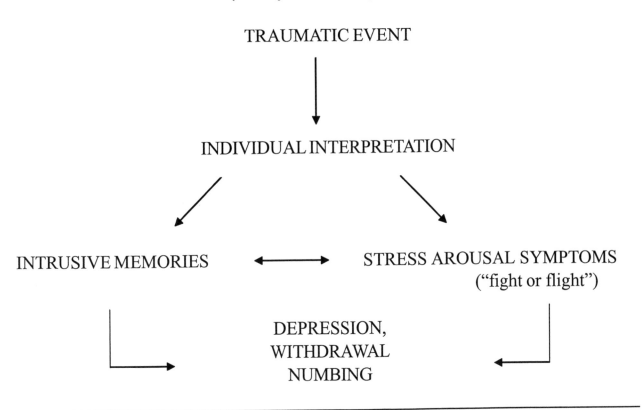

As described in Everly and Lating (1995) the manifestation of the three symptom clusters consisting of intrusive memories, stress arousal symptoms, and withdrawal, depression, and numbing are predicated upon a complex interaction between the traumatic event and the individual experiencing the event.

Figure 4

SUBJECTIVE INTERPRETATION AND EVENT POTENCY

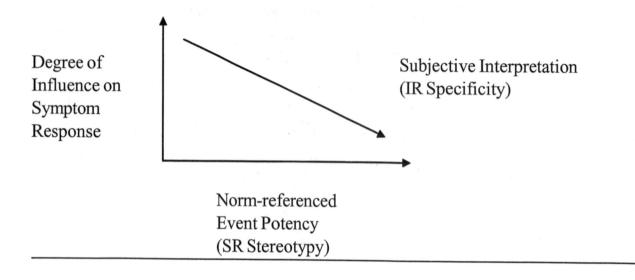

Degree of
Influence on
Symptom
Response

Subjective Interpretation
(IR Specificity)

Norm-referenced
Event Potency
(SR Stereotypy)

As noted in Figure 3, the nature and degree of manifest posttraumatic symptomatology is a function of the nature of the traumatic event and the individual experiencing the event. So as not to misinterpret this concept as reason to "blame the victim," Figure 4 above portrays the role of the victim's subjective interpretation in overall event potency (severity). Traumatic events will vary in their normative severity, or potency. This is called stimulus response stereotypy and simply means that "mild" stressors usually engender "mild" responses, while "severe" stressors usually engender "severe" responses. Automobile accidents are less severe than torture. Thus, as the norm-referenced severity of the stressor event increases, the less a role subjective interpretation, called individual response specificity, plays in determining the severity of the manifest symptom response. Thus, subjective interpretation pays less of a role in shaping the traumatic response to torture than it might be compared to an automobile accident.

Table 2

COMMON EGO DEFENSE MECHANISMS FOR
PSYCHOLOGICAL HOMEOSTASIS

ACTING OUT: Serves to prevent or ventilate accumulated tensions; e.g., stealing, lying, violence, etc.

DENIAL: Protection against a painful external reality; e.g., refusal to acknowledge awareness of stressful events.

DISPLACEMENT: Sustains a relationship in the context of discord / distress; e.g., transferring negative affect from one person, place, or thing to another as in phobic reactions.

DISSOCIATION: Protection against otherwise overwhelming realities; e.g., depersonalization, derealization.

INTELLECTUALIZATION: Protects against uncomfortable emotions; e.g., relating to and/or responding to affective material with cognitive responses.

INTROJECTION: Serves to create a protective enmeshment with another so as to derive a sense of protection; e.g., enmeshed overidentification / blending with another.

PASSIVE AGGRESSIVENESS: Protects against loss of control / power; e.g., duplicity, procrastination, "game playing."

PROJECTION: Protects against socially unacceptable behavior; e.g., projecting onto others feelings or motives of one's own.

RATIONALIZATION: Protects against disappointment, guilt, frustration; e.g., providing socially acceptable explanations for unacceptable behavior.

REGRESSION: Serves to create a less stressful, more neutral environment with lower expectations; e.g., dependency, thumb sucking, submissiveness.

REPRESSION: Protection against pain, discord, trauma; e.g., unconscious psychogenic amnesia.

RETREAT INTO FANTASY: Serves to relieve frustration by creating a safe environment for actions deemed too high risk to perform in reality; e.g., daydreaming, creation of a fantasy friend, etc.

SOMATIZATION: Protects against passivity and conflict; e.g., presentation of medically unexplainable symptoms in sensory or motor systems.

SUBLIMATION: Protects against guilt and frustration; e.g., channeling unacceptable urges into socially acceptable behavior.

SUPPRESSION: Same as above, except intentional effort to block recall.

UNDOING: Protects against threats; e.g., compulsive symbolic purification or neutralization of threat.

SIGNS AND SYMPTOMS OF DISTRESS

I. COGNITIVE (Thinking)
II. EMOTIONAL
III. BEHAVIORAL
IV. PHYSICAL
V. SPIRITUAL

DISTRESS (excessive stress).
Rx…Identify, Assess, & Monitor
vs.
DYSFUNCTION (impairment)
Rx…Identify, Assess, & Take
action

I. COGNITIVE (Thinking) DISTRESS

➢ Sensory Distortion
➢ Inability to Concentrate
➢ Difficulty in Decision Making
➢ Guilt
➢ Preoccupation (obsessions) with Event
➢ Confusion ("dumbing down")
➢ Inability to Understand Consequences of Behavior

I. SEVERE COGNITIVE DYSFUNCTION

- Suicidal/ Homicidal Ideation
- Paranoid Ideation
- Persistent Diminished Problem-solving
- Dissociation
- Disabling Guilt
- Hallucinations
- Delusions
- Persistent Hopelessness/ Helplessness

II. EMOTIONAL DISTRESS

- Anxiety
- Irritability
- Anger
- Mood Swings
- Depression
- Fear, Phobia, Phobic Avoidance
- Posttraumatic Stress (PTS)
- Grief

II. SEVERE EMOTIONAL DYSFUNCTION

- Panic Attacks
- Infantile Emotions in Adults
- Immobilizing Depression
- Posttraumatic Stress Disorder (PTSD)

Posttraumatic stress (PTS) is
a normal survival response;
Posttraumatic Stress Disorder
(PTSD) is a pathologic
variant of that
normal survival reaction.

PTSD

A. Traumatic event

B. Intrusive memories

C. Avoidance, numbing, depression

D. Stress arousal

E. Symptoms last > 30 days

F. Impaired functioning

Predicting PTSD

1. Dose - response relationship
   with exposure

2. Personal identification with
   event

3. Very important beliefs violated

PTSD results from violation of:

1. EXPECTATIONS

2. DEEPLY HELD BELIEFS
(Worldviews)

CORE BELIEFS (Worldviews)

- Belief in a just and fair world
- Need to trust others
- Self-esteem, Self-efficacy
- Need for a predictable and SAFE world
- Spirituality, belief in an order and congruence in life and the universe

---

Severity of PTSD

- Dissociation
- Psychogenic amnesia
- Persistent sleep disturbance
- Panic
- Severe exaggerated startle response
- Evidence of seizures

III. BEHAVIORAL DISTRESS

- Impulsiveness
- Risk-taking
- Excessive Eating
- Alcohol/ Drug Use
- Hyperstartle
- Compensatory Sexuality
- Sleep Disturbance
- Withdrawal
- Family Discord
- Crying Spells
- Hypervigilance
- 1000-yard Stare

III. SEVERE BEHAVIORAL DYSFUNCTION

- Violence
- Antisocial Acts
- Abuse of Others
- Diminished Personal Hygiene
- Immobility
- Self-medication

IV. PHYSICAL DISTRESS

- Tachycardia or Bradycardia
- Headaches
- Hyperventilation
- Muscle Spasms
- Psychogenic Sweating
- Fatigue / Exhaustion
- Indigestion, Nausea, Vomiting

IV. SEVERE PHYSICAL DYSFUNCTION

- Chest Pain
- Persistent Irregular Heartbeats
- Recurrent Dizziness
- Seizure
- Recurrent Headaches

IV. SEVERE PHYSICAL DYSFUNCTION

- Blood in vomit, urine, stool, sputum
- Collapse / loss of consciousness
- Numbness / paralysis (especially of arm, leg, face)
- Inability to speak / understand speech

It is imperative that all evidence of physical dysfunction be taken seriously and referred to a physician. The same is true when dealing with any physical distress that does not remit, may be suggestive of a medical disorder, or seems ambiguous.

V. SPIRITUAL DISTRESS

꙳Anger at God

꙳Withdrawal from Faith-based Community

꙳Crisis of Faith

V. SEVERE SPIRITUAL DYSFUNCTION

꙳Cessation from Practice of Faith

꙳Religious Hallucinations or Delusions

NOTE!

ALL OF THE SIGNS AND SYMPTOMS OF SEVERE DYSFUNCTION WARRANT REFERRAL TO THE NEXT LEVEL OF CARE!

Also refer whenever in doubt.

11 Screening Factors:

1. Ask about nature & severity of exposure
2. Ask about peri-traumatic dissociation — *around the incident*
3. Ask if person truly believed he / she was going to die
4. Ask about appraisal of symptoms (are they catastrophic?)
5. Physical injuries

11 Screening Factors:

6. Malignant sympathetic arousal – panic, loss of bowel or bladder control
7. Psychogenic amnesia — *not remembering the event*
8. Peri-traumatic depression, numbing
9. Self-destructive ideation
10. Evidence of psychotic process
11. Whenever in doubt!

FOR EXAMPLE
Have you recently . . .

1. Seen anyone seriously injured or killed? Or have you seen any type of human remains?

2. Felt as if you were in serious danger, or thought that you were going to die?

In the last couple of weeks, or so, have you…

3. Felt hopeless, helpless, or seriously depressed?

4. Felt numb or detached from the people you were with, your surroundings, or even from your usual bodily sensations?

_____

_____

_____

_____

_____

_____

5. Seriously thought about hurting yourself, or ending you own life?

6. Seriously thought about hurting or killing someone else?

7. Thought you were "going crazy?"

8. Experienced panic?

9. Experienced a crisis of spiritual, or religious, belief?

_____

_____

_____

_____

_____

10. Had difficulty getting along with close friends, family, or co-workers?

11. Used alcohol, or other substances specifically to help you relax or sleep?

12. Would you be interested in talking to someone about any of these, or other, concerns you might have?

_____

_____

_____

_____

_____

NOTES

MECHANISMS OF ACTION IN CRISIS INTERVENTION

Section VI

Remember Maslow's (1943) Need Hierarchy

- ↝Self – actualization
- ↝Self – esteem
- ↝Affiliation
- ↝Safety
- ↝Basic physical needs (START HERE)

PERSONALITY ALIGNMENT

COGNITIVE ORIENTATION
vs.
AFFECTIVE ORIENTATION

PSYCHOLOGICAL ALIGNMENT

- ↝Don't argue
- ↝Don't minimize problem
- ↝Find something to agree upon
- ↝Is the most important element in establishing rapport

MECHANISMS OF ACTION

(rec-Recommended; emp - Data based; rev - Review of literature)

- MEETING BASIC NEEDS (NIMH, 2002-rec)
- LIAISON / ADVOCACY (NIMH, 2002-rec
- CATHARTIC VENTILATION (Pennebaker, 1999-emp)
- SOCIAL SUPPORT, GROUP COHESION (Flannery, 1990-emp; APA, 2004-rec)
- INFORMATION (NIMH, 2002-rec)

MECHANISMS OF ACTION

(rec-Recommended; emp - Data based; rev - Review of literature)

- STRESS MANAGEMENT (Everly & Lating, 2002-rev)
- PROBLEM-SOLVING (Everly & Lating, 2002-rev)
- CONFLICT RESOLUTION (Everly & Lating, 2002-rev)
- COGNITIVE REFRAMING (Taylor, 1983-emp; Affleck & Tennen, 1996-rec)
- SPIRITUAL (Everly & Lating, 2002-rev)

AVOID!

- "I know how you feel."
- "It's not so bad."
- "This was God's will."
- "God won't give you more than you can handle."
- "Others have it much worse."

AVOID!

- "You need to forget about it."
- "You did the best you could."
  (Unless person has told you that.)
- "You really need to experience this pain."
- Psychotherapeutic interpretation!
- Confrontation
- Paradoxical intention.

EXERCISE

PRACTICE IN CRISIS
INTERVENTION
MECHANISMS

(Observer's Form #3)

SOME INTRODUCTORY THOUGHTS ON FORMULATING THE INTERVENTION

SIMPLICITY, PRAGMATISM AND INNOVATION

In beginning to develop a strategic intervention, several overarching points should be kept in mind:

1) Simple, problem-focused, pragmatic interventions are generally the most useful. As Rapoport (1965) noted, "A little help, rationally directed and purposefully focused at a strategic time is more effective than more extensive help given at a period of less emotional accessibility" (p. 30).

2) Pragmatism and innovation are the "keynotes" of successful crisis intervention (Slaby, Lieb & Tancredi, 1975). The intervention must, not only be a pragmatic, problem-focused intervention, but it must assume a dynamic plasticity in order to meet the challenges of a crisis situation, many of which may be latent.

CRISIS AS A TOXIN

Using the simile of crisis as a toxin allows us to introduce several simple, yet important, intervention concepts.

1. A calm, reassuring approach is an antidote for anxiety.
2. Structure is an antidote for chaos.
3. Thinking is an antidote for dysfunctional emotions.
4. Catharsis is an antidote for psychological tension and frustration.
5. Information is an antidote for loss of control.
6. Acceptance and social support are antidotes for alienation.
7. Action is an antidote for helplessness.

CRISIS INTERVENTION IS NOT PSYCHOTHERAPY

An important element in crisis intervention is remembering that crisis intervention is NOT psychotherapy. While it certainly contains psychotherapeutic elements, it is not therapy as practiced by licensed mental health clinicians. It may be thought of as a form of emotional first-aid. Thus, as physical first-aid is to the practice of medicine, crisis intervention is to the practice of psychotherapy.

Three key pillars upon which crisis intervention differs from psychotherapy are: 1) immediacy, 2) proximity and, 3) expectancy (Solomon & Benbenishty, 1986).

FORMULATING AN APPROACH TO A PERSON IN CRISIS

In any crisis situation, in any negotiation, in any exercise in rhetoric, in any meaningful human exchange, it is useful to understand, as best you can, the psychological style, or nature, of the person with whom you are communicating. Noted personologist, Theodore Millon (1996) has developed the most comprehensive model of personologic styles used today. In one aspect of his formulations, he notes that there are two diametrically opposed styles of information processing that human beings may employ. Using this perspective, it may be suggested that there are two different types of people: 1) cognitively oriented people and, 2) affectively oriented people.

Cognitively oriented people use reason and logic preferentially. Their favored ego defense mechanism is often denial. When in crisis, their first response is to attempt problem-solving. Later, they may be seen to withdraw into themselves, or "shut-down." The crisis worker's attempts at intervention may be perceived as **intrusive** and **insensitive** if not implemented cautiously. **Avoid** authoritarian or confrontational approaches. Once it is determined that the person in crisis is medically stable and of no threat to self or others, the crisis worker should offer to assist in the problem-solving mode, if appropriate. Cognitively oriented individuals will usually prosper from information. For them information is usually an anxiolytic, or it may serve to assist in the problem-solving efforts and action plan formulation. If no direct action seems indicated, the crisis worker should provide an opportunity for cathartic ventilation. If the person in crisis resists this offer, it is usually best for the crisis worker to provide the person in crisis with some psychological "distance" while still communicating the desire to be supportive. Such support is typically best received when the person in crisis is "ready."

Affectively oriented people will usually prosper from affectively-based crisis interventions. Such interventions include acceptance, validation, a supportive presence, cathartic ventilation and even abreactive states. Affectively oriented individuals may have an even greater expectation for ameliorative action on the part of the crisis worker, when compared to the cognitively oriented person and they will be less likely to expeditiously act on their own behalf in a problem solving mode. They typically will not feel disenfranchised if the crisis worker "solves" the problem. That is not to say, however, that this personality is immune from feeling intruded upon by an excessively direct, authoritarian, or confrontational intervention approach. Thus, both personality types may become iatrogenically defensive or "shut down" as a result of an excessively vigorous approach.

OBSERVER'S FEEDBACK FORM
#3
<u>Role Play Exercise</u>

1. Use of silence:

2. Body language / posture conducive to communication:

3. Appropriate choice of verbal language:

4. Use of restatement:

5. Use of emotional reflection:

6. Use of paraphrasing:
   a) Summary:

   b) Extrapolation:

7. Use of open-ended questions:

8. Use of closed-ended questions:

9. Did the crisis worker use an effective introduction?__YES; __NO
    What improvements could be made?

10. Did the intervention follow a structure or appear to have a plan? __YES;__NO
    What improvements could be made?

11. Did it appear as if the intervention would be effective?__YES;__NO
    What improvements could be made?

12. What evidence, if any, was there of:
    a) Transference?

    b) Countertransference?

NOTES

DO NO HARM!

Section VII

CRISIS = RESPONSE

The failure to understand that the event is NOT the crisis, can easily lead to over intervention, and the potential to interfere with natural recovery mechanisms!

CAN INTERVENTION BE HARMFUL ?
The Case of Psychotherapy...

- Smith, Glass, & Miler (Benefits of Psychotherapy, 1980) meta-analytic review of 400 studies --> 9% negative outcome
- Shapiro & Shapiro (Psychol. Bulletin, 1982) over 1800 "effects" --> 11% negative, 30% null
- Lambert (2003) estimated 5-10% of patients deteriorate during treatment

---

ROLE OF PSYCHOLOGICAL THERAPY

- Crisis intervention and psychological therapy are opposite ends of the same continuum of care

- Cognitive Behavior Therapy (CBT) and its core exposure element has shown great promise. Other psychotherapeutic models (e.g., EMDR,) also seem applicable.

HOWEVER, CBT exposure component may be contraindicated with the following crises and disaster related conditions:

- extreme anxiety & panic

- marked dissociation

- psychosis

- severe depression

- suicidal risk, homicidal risk

- anger

HOWEVER, CBT exposure component may be contraindicated with the following crises and disaster related conditions:

- unresolved prior trauma

- ongoing stressors

- acute bereavement (Bryant & Harvey, Acute Stress Disorder, 2000, pp.145-146)

- CBT studies may have drop-out rates as high as 29% (Foa et al., 2002, cited in McNally, Bryant, Ehlers, 2003)

CAN PSYCHOTHERAPY BE HARMFUL ?
DROP-OUT FROM PSYCHOTHERAPY

- CBT studies may have drop-out rates as high as 29% (Foa et al., 2002, cited in McNally, Bryant, Ehlers, 2003)

- Exposure alone: 20.5%

- Stress Inoculation Training or Cognitive Therapy alone: 22.1%

CAN PSYCHOTHERAPY BE HARMFUL ?
DROP-OUT FROM PSYCHOTHERAPY

≈ Exposure plus SIT or CT: 26.9%

≈ EMDR: 18.9%

≈ Relaxation "control" conditions: ~7%

≈ Wait list controls: ~11% (compiled within Hembree, et al, JTS, 2003)

CAN CRISIS INTERVENTION BE HARMFUL ?
Theoretical Mechanisms/ Issues
(see Dyregrov, IJEMH, 1999; Watson, et al., in Ursano & Norwood, 2003)

≈ Excessive catharsis, disclosure, rumination

≈ Pathologizing otherwise "normal" reactions

≈ Vicarious traumatization in groups

≈ Coercive peer pressure in groups

≈ Scapegoating in groups

CAN CRISIS INTERVENTION BE HARMFUL ?
Theoretical Mechanisms/ Issues
(see Dyregrov, IJEMH, 1999; Watson, et al., in Ursano & Norwood, 2003)

≈ Triggering of previous traumatic memories

≈ Intervention may be premature (inappropriate timing)

≈ May be inappropriate with highly aroused persons

≈ May interfere with natural coping mechanisms

≈ May not be accompanied by adequate assessment or follow-up

CAUTION!

It is important for the interventionist to keep in mind the following points:

1. The majority of individuals exposed to a traumatic event will not need formal psychological intervention, beyond being provided relevant information.
2. The focus should be upon the *individual* more so than the event; assessment is essential. Assessment is an on-going dynamic process, rather than a discrete, static stage.
3. Normalization of the crisis response is to be encouraged, but should never lead one to dismiss serious crisis reactions.

CAUTION!

It is important for the interventionist to keep in mind the following points:

4. Unless the magnitude of impairment is such that the individual represents a threat to self or others, crisis intervention should be voluntary.
5. The interventionist must be careful not to interfere with natural recovery or adaptive compensatory mechanisms.
6. The potential for vicarious traumatization must be reduced.
7. Individuals should not be encouraged to talk about or relive the event, unless they are comfortable doing so.
8. When in doubt, seek assistance, supervision.

The risk of adverse outcome is associated with all human intervention and helping practices including medicine, surgery and counseling.

Improper, inadequate training would appear the greatest risk factor associated with crisis intervention, as well as those practices just mentioned.

Thus, training and supervision may be the best way to reduce the risk of adverse outcome, rather than simply calling for an end to such helping practices

REVIEW:

"Early Psychological
Intervention:
A Word of Caution"

NOTES

SAFER-REVISED MODEL OF INDIVIDUAL CRISIS INTERVENTION

Section VIII

A PROTOCOL FOR WORKING WITH INDIVIDUALS IN CRISIS

Effectively aiding an individual in crisis usually requires more than merely allowing that individual to engage in cathartic ventilation. Effective crisis intervention usually requires a plan, or protocol, to serve as a general guide for intervention.

In 1993, Mitchell and Everly (1993), wrote a seminal text on the use of group crisis intervention techniques. This text provided detailed intervention protocols for small, as well as large, groups. The group intervention protocols were for the intervention techniques of small group defusings, Critical Incident Stress Debriefings (CISD), and large group demobilizations (see Mitchell and Everly, 1993).

Interestingly, most crisis intervention is done individually, one-on-one. So, as there was a need for group crisis intervention protocols, there is a need for crisis intervention protocol for working with individuals. That protocol is referred to as the SAFER-R model and is presented in this section.

SAFER-R Model of Crisis Intervention with Individuals
(Everly, 2001)

Stabilization (plus Introduction) [1]

Acknowledgement [1]

A. Event

B. Reactions

Facilitation of Understanding: Normalization [1]

Encourage Effective Coping (Mechanisms of Action) [1,2,3]

Referral? [1, 2, 3]

[1= Assessment, 2= Generate intervention options, 3= Implement interventions]

SAFER-R Model of Crisis Intervention with Individuals
(Everly, 2001)

Stabilization (plus Introduction) [1]

Acknowledgement [1]

A. Event

B. Reactions

Facilitation of Understanding: Normalization [1]

Encourage Effective Coping (Mechanisms of Action) [1,2,3]

MEETING BASIC NEEDS

LIAISON/ ADVOCACY

CATHARTIC VENTILATION

SOCIAL SUPPORT

INFORMATION

STRESS MANAGEMENT

PROBLEM-SOLVING

CONFLICT RESOLUTION

COGNITIVE REFRAMING

SPIRITUAL

Referral? [1, 2, 3]

[1= Assessment, 2= Generate intervention options, 3= Implement interventions]

Crisis Intervention applications can be made easier by the utilization of simple models. The SAFER-R model is nothing more than a step-by-step model for working with individuals in crisis

The SAFER-Revised

- Stabilize (introduction; meet basic needs; mitigate acute stressors)
- Acknowledge the crisis (event, reactions)
- Facilitate understanding (normalization)
- Encourage effective coping (mechanisms of action)
- Recovery or Referral (facilitate access to continued care)

SAFER-R Model of Crisis Intervention with Individuals (Everly, 2001)

Stabilization (plus Introduction) [1]

⬇

Acknowledgement [1]
A. Event
B. Reactions

⬇

Facilitation of Understanding: Normalization [1]

⬇

Encourage Effective Coping (Mechanisms of Action) [1,2,3]

⬇

Referral? [1, 2, 3]

[1= Assessment, 2= Generate intervention options, 3= Implement interventions]

SAFER-R Model of Crisis Intervention with Individuals
(Everly, 2001)

Stabilization (plus Introduction) [1]

↓

Acknowledgement [1]
A. Event
B. Reactions

↓

Facilitation of Understanding: Normalization [1]

↓

Encourage Effective Coping (Mechanisms of Action) [1,2,3]
MEETING BASIC NEEDS
LIAISON/ ADVOCACY
CATHARTIC VENTILATION
SOCIAL SUPPORT
INFORMATION
STRESS MANAGEMENT
PROBLEM-SOLVING
CONFLICT RESOLUTION
COGNITIVE REFRAMING
SPIRITUAL

↓

Referral? [1, 2, 3]
[1= Assessment, 2= Generate intervention options, 3= Implement interventions]

AN EXAMPLE

- Introduce yourself

- Meet basic needs, stabilize, liaison

- Listen to the "story" (events, reactions)

- Reflect emotion

- Paraphrase content

AN EXAMPLE

- Normalize

- Attribute reactions to situation, not personal weakness

- Identify personal stress management tools to empower

- Identify external support / coping resources

- Use problem-solving or cognitive reframing, if applicable

- Assess person's ability to safely function

SUICIDE: A SPECIAL CASE

- Helplessness
- Hopelessness
- Extreme guilt
- Previous attempts
- Severe illness, disability
- Psychosis

SUICIDE: C-C-D-R Intervention

- CLARIFY
- CONTRADICT
- DELAY
- REFER for continued to care

SUICIDE INTERVENTION

- CLARIFY: "Do you really want to die, or do you simply want to change the way you live your life?

- CONTRADICT via:
  - Desired outcome will not be achieved
  - Suicide will create more problems than it solves
  - Suicide creates an adverse and undesired "ripple effect" affecting others

SUICIDE INTERVENTION

≈●DELAY

≈●ALWAYS ASSIST IN ACCESSING
HIGHER LEVEL OF CARE

SAFER-R Model of Crisis Intervention with Individuals:
Modified for Suicide Intervention
(Everly, 2001)

Stabilization (plus Introduction) [1]

⬇

Acknowledgement [1]
A. Event
B. Reactions

⬇

Facilitation of Understanding: Normalization [1]

⬇

Encourage Effective Coping (Mechanisms of Action) [1,2,3]
CLARIFY, CONTRADICT, DELAY

⬇

Referral...ALWAYS! [1, 2, 3]
[1= Assessment, 2= Generate intervention options, 3= Implement interventions]

SOME SPECIAL CHALLENGES

THE NONCOMMUNICATIVE PERSON

- For many individuals, a common psychological response to crisis is to psychologically and behaviorally withdraw. This withdrawal is often underscored by a noncommunicative posture.

- When approaching someone who is noncommunicative, it is imperative that one rule out any medical conditions that would interfere with communication. Physical shock, head injury, hypoglycemia, hypothermia and dissociative states are serious conditions that should be referred for acute medical care.

- Once ruling out these and any related conditions, the crisis worker should approach the noncommunicative individual with the goal of achieving what is in the person's best interest, not necessarily getting the person to communicate, although this is usually helpful.

- Beginning with a reflection technique can be useful, "You look like you're having a hard time with this one." Following up with an offer to help may be of further value, "What can I do to help you right now?"

- If the person in crisis expresses a desire to be left alone, it is usually a good idea to offer one more time then acquiesce to the request, if you believe the person is no threat to self or others. If you are not sure, it may be a good idea to remain in somewhat close proximity. Remember, it is possible for the crisis worker to be perceived as intrusive or insensitive if you do not honor one's request for solitude or privacy. This may result in hostility being expressed toward the crisis worker. Or, it may drive the person in crisis deeper into psychological retreat.

- On the other hand, it is irresponsible to leave someone alone who is questionably capable of independent functioning. Thus, the crisis worker should not leave an emotionally impaired individual until that person is no longer impaired or is turned over to the care of someone of equal or greater professional competence than the crisis worker.

THE DAZED OR NONRESPONSIVE PERSON

- Upon occasion, the crisis worker will encounter individuals who seems "dazed" or otherwise nonresponsive. They seem to simply stare out into space.

- The first task is to insure that this person is medically stable. The crisis worker must do the best he / she can do to rule out medical origins for the nonresponsive state. Factors such as toxins, hypoglycemia, blood loss, drug reactions and closed or open head injury must be ruled out or attended to prior to any psychotherapeutic tactic being initiated.

- The classic psychogenic nonresponsive state may have several potential mechanisms of action:
1) a parasympathetically – mediated "spill-over effect";
2) a vegetative depressive syndrome;
3) feelings of being overwhelmed, leading to acute attentional deficits, helpless and / or hopeless perceptions;
4) extreme physical and / or psychological fatigue; and,
5) peritraumatic dissociation.

- The reader is referred to the section on the **noncommunicative person** for suggestions on how to approach the nonresponsive individual.

- When dealing with the nonresponsive individual, it is even more imperative that is person not be left alone. Silent supportive attendance should be maintained for up to an hour. Should the symptoms persist, consideration should be given to taking the person in crisis to an emergency room or some qualified health practitioner for assessment.

Book to Read
The Wisdom of Listening

Homework
Create scenario
I.O. target + focus groups you would need
to address in your scenario
2 or 3 role for 1 on 1 roleplay

THE EMOTIONAL TIRADE

- Both individual and group crisis interventions, such as the CISD, are vulnerable to individuals embarking upon emotional tirades. It is imperative that the crisis worker attempt to de-escalate the tirade before it spirals out of control, or ignites similar behavior in others.

- The reflection technique can be used to reflect back to the person in crisis the nature of their expressed emotion. "You seem really angry, right now." Once acknowledging the expressed emotion, the crisis worker may then attempt to shift the context from the affective domain to the cognitive domain by asking a follow-up question such as "What's causing you to react like this?" This tactic serves as a useful transition, or bridge, into a problem-solving mode.

- If possible, the intervention ends in the development of a plan to reduce the distress manifested earlier in the tirade. The plan should focus, as much as possible, upon generating solutions to the problem that engendered the emotional response in the first place.

If no such solutions are available, per se, then the focus of the plan becomes generating alternatives for easing the acute distress and for coping with the intractable situation.

THE VERBALLY ABUSIVE PERSON

- Occasionally, the crisis worker will be the target of verbal abuse from the person experiencing the acute crisis. Often times, an argument will be initiated that seems illogical or irrelevant.

- Once again, the reflection technique is a useful way to start the intervention.

- However, as the verbiage becomes increasingly hostile or irrelevant, it becomes imperative that the crisis worker not fall into the trap of arguing with the person in crisis.

- Rather, at this point it is useful to employ a "content to process shift." The function of this intervention is to shift the discussion away from an argument about a set of "facts" which you can never win (content), to a discussion of the "process" of the argument itself.

- This technique is useful, not only with angry individuals, but with noncommunicative individuals, as well. In such cases, the crisis worker would comment upon the manifest anger, the reticence, etc.

EXERCISE

PRACTICE IN SAFER-Revised

(Observer's Form #4)

OBSERVER'S FEEDBACK FORM
#4
SAFER Role Play Exercise

1. Use of silence:

2. Body language / posture conducive to communication:

3. Appropriate choice of verbal language:

4. Use of restatement:

5. Use of emotional reflection:

6. Use of paraphrasing:
   a) Summary:

   b) Extrapolation:

7. Use of open-ended questions:

8. Use of closed-ended questions:

9. Did the crisis worker use an effective introduction?__YES; __NO
    What improvements could be made?

10. Did the intervention follow a structure or appear to have a plan? __YES;__NO
    What improvements could be made?

11. Did it appear as if the intervention would be effective?__YES;__NO
    What improvements could be made?

12. What evidence, if any, was there of:
    a) Transference?

    b) Countertransference?

COMMONLY USED CRISIS AND DISASTER MENTAL HEALTH INTERVENTIONS

Appendix A

PRE-INCIDENT PREPARATION

- Assessment of risk
- Risk reduction
- Assessment of physical and psychological response preparedness
- Training to reduce vulnerabilities
- Training to create "resistance"
- Training to enhance "resilience" and response capabilities

ASSESSMENT

One element often left out of crisis intervention is acute assessment, e.g., mental status, behavioral assessment, the Johns Hopkins' "perspectives," etc.

ALL Crisis Intervention should be based upon the Assessment of NEED…and the further ASSESSMENT of the most appropriate intervention.

A strategic planning model may assist in this process.

STRATEGIC PLANNING FORMULA

1. THREAT

2. TARGET (Who should receive services? ID target groups.)

3. **TYPE** (What interventions should be used?)

STRATEGIC PLANNING FORMULA

4. **TIMING** (When should the interventions be implemented, with what target groups?)

5. **RESOURCES** (What intervention resources are available to be mobilized for what target groups, when? Consider internal and external resources.)

[Note: **THEMES** which may modify impact and response should be considered (children, chem-bio hazards, etc?)]

DEMOBILIZATION

A one time, large-group information process for emergency services, military or other operations staff who have been exposed to a significant significant traumatic event such as a disaster or terrorist event

RESPITE/ REHAB SECTORS

Ongoing physical & psychosocial
decompression (respite) areas constructed
at the disaster venue to provide support
(beverages, light food, protection from
weather, and provision of psychological
support / stress management) typically to
emergency personnel.

CRISIS MANAGEMENT BRIEFINGS (CMB)
(Everly, 2000)
Structured large group (can be used in small
groups, as well) community / organizational
"town meetings" designed to provide
information about the incident, control
rumors, educate about symptoms of distress,
inform about basic stress management, and
identify resources available for continued
support, if desired. Especially useful in
response to violence / terrorism.

DEFUSINGS

Small group (< 20) structured
3-phase group discussion regarding a
critical incident.
Typically done with homogeneous
work groups usually within 12 hours
of the event.
May be repeated for ongoing events.

"DEBRIEFING"

The term "debriefing" has been used frequently in the theory and practice of crisis intervention.

Used within the context of CISM, the term "debriefing" refers to a 7 - phase structured small group crisis intervention more specifically named Critical Incident Stress Debriefing (CISD).

CRITICAL INCIDENT STRESS DEBRIEFING (CISD)
(Mitchell & Everly, 2001)

A structured 7-phase group discussion typically conducted with homogeneous groups 2 - 10 days (3+ weeks in mass disasters) post incident.

Designed to mitigate distress, facilitate psychological closure, or facilitate access to continued care.

In 1983, Mitchell's original paper used the term CISD to refer to both the overarching response system and the small group discussion.
This resulted in semantic confusion.
Now, the term Critical Incident Stress Management (CISM) is used to denote the overarching response system, while CISD is used to refer to the 7-phase small group discussion.

The term "debriefing," when used alone, has been used in so many different ways, it has lost its meaning and adds to confusion.

For example, research from the UK often uses the term debriefing to describe 1:1 counseling with medical patients.

Unfortunately, some reviews and studies have used the term debriefing to describe such forms of counseling. Further, the Cochrane Review has been inappropriately cited as evidence of the ineffectiveness of all forms of "debriefing," even group CISD!

INDIVIDUAL (1:1) INTERVENTION

Most crisis intervention is done individually, one-on-one,
either face-to-face or telephonically.

Psychological first aid (PFA) is the most elemental form of this intervention

FAMILY CRISIS INTERVENTION

Traumatic distress can be "contagious;"
family members are often adversely affected
by those who initially develop posttraumatic
distress.
AND
Families of victims require support,
especially when loved ones are seriously
injured or killed.

ORGANIZATIONAL /
COMMUNITY
CRISIS RESPONSE

Consists of risk assessment, pre- and post
incident strategic planning,
tactical training and intervention,
consultation with leadership, and the
development of a comprehensive crisis plan.

PASTORAL
CRISIS INTERVENTION (PCI)

The functional integration of the
principles and practices of
psychological crisis intervention
with the principles and practices of
pastoral support.
(Everly, IJEMH, 2000)

FOLLOW-UP & REFERRAL

All forms of crisis intervention should possess some form of follow-up.
In addition, one of the most cogent reasons for instituting a crisis intervention program is to identify those who require or
desire continued care, and to facilitate access to that care.

REMEMBER!

CISD / CISM are not substitutes for psychotherapy.
Rather, they are elements within the emergency mental health system designed to precede and complement psychotherapy,
i.e., part of the full continuum of care.

NOTES

BACKGROUND
PAPERS

Appendix
B

The Evolving Nature of Disaster Mental Health Services

George S. Everly, Jr., and Alan Langlieb

ABSTRACT: *It may be said that the field of emergency/disaster mental health is a mental health sub-specialization that continues, even today, to quantitatively expand and qualitatively evolve. For this evolutionary process to continue successfully, greater sophistication must be realized both tactically, as well as strategically. This paper reviews the evolving nature of crisis intervention and emergency/disaster mental health. Three areas will be reviewed herein: the evolving goals of early intervention, tactical evolution, and the evolving nature of training in emergency/disaster mental health.*

KEY WORDS: *disaster mental health, crisis intervention, Critical Incident Stress Management (CISM), training*

Although the field of psychological crisis intervention has existed since the early 1900s, the field of disaster mental health appears to have developed far more recently, in the early 1990s. The development of this field was due to a confluence of numerous factors, such as the recognition of the mental health consequences of mass disasters, an increase in global terrorism, the advent of the disaster mental health networks of the American Red Cross, the expanding presence of intervention teams from the National Organization for Victims' Assistance (NOVA), the proliferation of Critical Incident Stress Management (CISM) teams affiliated with the International Critical Incident Stress Foundation (ICISF), and the expansion of the Salvation Army's services to include disaster mental health. These factors served to herald and similarly facilitate the growth and evolution of this new field. *But it must be remembered that the initial development of any field is an imperfect process. As a result, it would* be expected that both tactical and strategic modifications should naturally occur over time and when confronted by challenging field applications. Responding to mass disasters such as Hurricane Andrew, Hurricane Iniki, the Mississippi River floods, the emergency mental health needs of post-war Kuwait and post-war Croatia, the Oklahoma City bombing, the terrorist attack on the *USS Cole*, the attacks of September 11, 2001, threats of bioterrorism, warfare in the Middle East, and even the snipers that plagued Washington, D.C., in 2002 and West Virginia in 2003, the field of emergency/disaster mental health has experienced changes in both tactical implementation and strategic planning.

Tactically, many interventions have undergone reconsideration and operational alterations since their initial development. Similarly, they have become increasingly innovative in order to respond to the plethora of situational complexities often associated with mass disasters.

Strategically, mass disasters and warfare demand the most sophisticated levels of strategic planning for the disaster mental health response. This due to the confluence of multi-dimensional needs demanding an integrated multi-faceted mental health response all housed within a structured Incident Command System (ICS). This paper will review the evolving nature of emergency/disaster mental health.

George S. Everly, Jr., Ph.D., The Johns Hopkins University, Bloomberg School of Public Health; Loyola College in Maryland; and the International Critical Incident Stress Foundation; and Alan Langlieb, M.D., M.P.H., M.B.A., The Johns Hopkins University School of Medicine. Address correspondence concerning this article to: George Everly, Jr., 702 Severnside Ave., Severna Park, MD 21146 USA.

Evolving Goals For Early Psychological Intervention

Setting appropriate goals for psychological crisis intervention (more recently referred to as emergency/disaster mental health) must be based upon a realistic formulation of what crisis intervention is and is not. Conceptually, a parallel may be drawn between physical health and mental health such that "as physical first aid is to surgery, psychological crisis intervention is to psychotherapy." As the goals of physical first aid are: (1) stabilization of physiological functioning, (2) mitigation of physiological dysfunction/distress, (3) return of acute adaptive physiological functioning, and/or (4) facilitation of access to the next level of care.

The goals of early psychological crisis intervention are: (1) stabilization of psychological functioning through meeting basic physical needs, then addressing the most basic of psychological needs, (2) mitigation of psychological dysfunction/distress, (3) return of acute adaptive psychological functioning, and/or (4) facilitation of access to the next level of care.

Psychological crisis intervention is not psychotherapy, nor is it a substitute for psychotherapy. Deahl (2000) has argued that early psychological intervention research is contaminated with the assumption that the outcome goals (and thereby, the expectations) for early psychological intervention are commonly confused with the same outcome goals of "treatment." Thus, the eradication of posttraumatic stress disorder (PTSD) may be an unfair expectation.

More specifically, as early psychological interventions such as disaster mental health initiatives were being originally formulated, lofty or overly simplistic expectations were sometimes implicitly, or explicitly applied. Initially, some believed that early psychological disaster response might exert a preventative effect so as to block the development of PTSD and other psychiatric reactions such as major depression (Mitchell & Everly, 1993; Everly, 1995). Research has yet to convincingly demonstrate such a global preventative effect (Arendt and Elklit, 2001; Professional Practice Board Working Party, 2002). Arendt and Elklit (2001), in a review of over two dozen controlled trials of early psychological intervention (generically referred to as "debriefing"), concluded that the prevention of PTSD seems an inappropriate expectation and a potential disservice to the field of early psychological intervention, with the possible exception of when such interventions are utilized with emergency services personnel. Again, the eradication of PTSD would seem an inappropriate expectation. A more appropriate outcome,

however, might be the ability to perform a screening function, as well as the *mitigation* of posttraumatic distress. Ursano, et al. (2003) note, "Multiple outcomes are of importance following disasters and terrorism and need to be examined for various types of interventions.... Interventions that foster return of function, even though they may not directly prevent psychiatric illness, may be of importance" (p. 336). Deahl and his colleagues (Deahl, et al., 2001; Deahl, 2000) have similarly argued that expectations for early psychological intervention should not be focused solely upon PTSD. They noted that early psychological intervention may positively affect other aspects of posttraumatic illness (PTI) that typically go unmeasured. They cite in support of such a conclusion their own randomized controlled trial of early intervention (specifically, CISD) which found a reduction of posttraumatic alcohol use in soldiers returning from a peace-keeping mission in eastern Europe (Deahl, et al., 2000). Interestingly, Flannery and his colleagues have developed an integrated CISM intervention program, referred to as ASAP, which has consistently shown effectiveness in reducing patient assaults upon institutional hospital staff (Flannery, 1999, 2001; Flannery, Hanson, Penk, Flannery, & Gallagher, 1995; Flannery, Penk, & Corrigan, 1999). According to Caplan (1964), the seminal writer in the field of modern psychological crisis intervention, a reasonable expectation for "prevention" would include *mitigation of symptoms, the reduction of dysfunction, and even the fostering of healthy coping behaviors.*

Tactical Evolution: Critical Incident Stress Management (CISM) As A Case Study

One of the earliest of the integrated multi-component psychological crisis intervention systems that has gained wide-spread utilization is CISM. The American Red Cross, the National Organization for Victims Assistance (NOVA), and the Salvation Army also utilize their own integrated, multi-component, crisis intervention systems. Early on, the British Psychological Society (1990) suggested that crisis intervention would likely be ineffective unless provided as a multi-component system. Historically, there has been some confusion as to the actual nature and evolution of the CISM approach to crisis intervention vis-à-vis the frequently utilized small group crisis intervention known as CISD, as well as numerous other crisis interventions generically referred to as "debriefing." A brief review of the evolution of CISM may prove useful in understanding the evolution of the field of emergency/disaster mental health. Additionally it may

---

serve to correct possible misconceptions and inappropriate expectations for the entire field.

CISM represents, both strategically and tactically, an integrated multi-faceted approach to crisis intervention. Consistent with Theodore Millon's (Millon, Grossman, Meagher, Millon, & Everly, 1999) concepts of *potentiating pairings* (using interacting combinations of interventions so as to achieve an enhancing clinical effect), *catalytic sequences* (sequentially combining tactical interventions in their most clinically useful ways), and the *polythetic nature* of the CISM approach (selecting the tactical interventions as determined by the specific needs of each crisis situation), specific crisis interventions within the CISM formulation are to be combined and sequenced in such a manner so as to yield the most efficient and effective crisis intervention possible. The various combinations and permutations that are actually utilized within the CISM model will be determined by the specific needs of each critical incident or traumatic event as they uniquely arise (Everly & Mitchell, 1999). The current integrated, multi-component nature of CISM was not commonly practiced, nor was it fully developed, in its formative years. Excessive reliance was placed upon one specific small group crisis intervention component of the overall CISM formulation. An over-utilization of the CISD intervention seemed clearly in evidence. Such an over-utilization of CISD was not to be unexpected, however.

Originally, Mitchell (1983) used the term CISD as an overarching label to refer to a strategic multi-componential approach to crisis intervention which contained four elements: (1) individual or group *on-scene* crisis intervention, (2) an initial post-incident small group discussion referred to as a "defusing," (3) a more formalized post-incident six-phase small group discussion referred to as the "formal CISD," and (4) follow-up psychological support services. As can be imagined, the author's use of the term CISD to denote: (1) the overarching strategic approach to crisis intervention, as well as, (2) a "formal" small group discussion process led to significant confusion, which persists even today. As a direct result of the confusion created by the dual usage of the term CISD, and more importantly the inferred, but erroneous, tacit endorsement of CISD (the small group discussion) as a singular stand-alone crisis intervention, the term CISD, as the label for the cumulative strategic crisis intervention system, was abandoned in favor of the term CISM (Everly & Mitchell, 1999).

More recently, then, the term CISD has been reserved exclusively for a seven-phase small group (roughly 3 to 20 participants) discussion designed to facilitate "psychological closure" (i.e., psychological progression beyond fixation upon the traumatic event) subsequent to a critical incident or traumatic event for primary, secondary, and even tertiary victims. A fact that is often overlooked in the scrutiny of CISD is that while CISD requires participants to meet in a group format, inherent in the CISD process itself is the explicit component of individual follow-up at some point after the end of the CISD and even the facilitation of access to a higher level of psychological support (Mitchell, 1983; Mitchell & Everly, 1993, 2001). Thus by definition, CISD was not intended to be a singular, stand-alone process.

Having reviewed the evolution of the term CISM, let us now review the core components of the CISM model (Mitchell & Everly, 2001; Everly & Mitchell, 1999), while noting their evolutionary trajectories. This list of components has been significantly modified from a tactical perspective and has been strategically expanded since originally introduced. The expansion of CISM has been a direct result of its utilization beyond its original role serving emergency services personnel subsequent to well circumscribed critical incidents and its more recent applications to mass disasters, military venues, and terrorist-related situations. It may be argued that such tactical modification and strategic expansion represents the avoidance of stagnation and is an imperative dynamic for a healthy system. The ten extant core CISM elements are listed below:

(1) *Pre-incident preparation and training.* This component of the CISM crisis intervention system refers to the processes of psychological and behavioral preparation designed to assist individuals in adjusting to an anticipated critical incident, or traumatic event prior to its actual occurrence.

Historically, this element of CISM was conspicuous in it absence. More specifically, crisis intervention services were almost exclusively reactionary in nature. This element represents a proactive step in emergency mental health. Notions of psychological immunization and "psychological body armor" are engendered by the introduction of this intervention to the pre-incident phase of the critical incident temporal continuum. Perhaps the most recent evolution in pre-incident preparation would be the addition of specialized training in the emerging field of "psychological counterterrorism" (Everly & Castellano, in press). Such an initiative has already begun within the law enforcement profession.

(2) *Demobilization.* Demobilizations represent an event driven approach to crisis intervention often used for public

safety, rescue, and emergency services personnel subsequent to a large scale crisis or disaster. Developed by Mitchell (see Mitchell & Everly, 1993) to mitigate stress reactions in large groups of emergency response personnel who might be secondary victims of trauma, the demobilization is a combination of physical nourishment and stress management education.

Historically, the demobilization was an opportunity for temporary psychological "decompression" immediately after exposure to a critical incident typically applied at the point of shift disengagement. While rooted in military psychiatry (Artiss, 1963; Salmon, 1919), the concepts of providing physical rest, nutrition, and psychoeducation have been employed and expanded through the development of the "respite" center. Respite centers have been utilized in response to sustained rescue and recovery operations in the wake of mass disasters. The American Red Cross pioneered the extant model of an ongoing respite center in their response to the World Trade Center terrorist attacks

(3) *Crisis Management Briefing.* The "crisis management briefing" (CMB) (Everly, 2000a) represents a form of "town meeting" or assembly designed to facilitate social support, mitigate the spread of dysfunctional rumors, and provide functional empowering information for large groups (up to 300 at a time). This event-driven intervention attempts to achieve these goals almost exclusively through the provision of information to those groups affected by the event.

Historically, this intervention was referred to as a "group informational briefing" (Everly & Mitchell, 1999), the process was refined and later referred to as the CMB (Everly, 2000a). It appears to be suited not only for mass disasters but for business and industrial applications, schools (Newman, 2000), and large-scale, community critical incidents such as violence, terrorist activities, and any other community adversity. The CMB may be used in military applications as well. This intervention may be done within hours of the crisis event and may be repeated as often as necessary. The CMB was employed by the New York City Police Department in the wake of September 11. A much larger and longer (two days) variation of the CMB was employed by the Port Authority Police of New York and New Jersey, also subsequent to the terrorist attacks of September 11, 2001.

(4) *Defusing.* One variation on the theme of small group (<20 individuals) crisis intervention is the "defusing." Defusings are 20-30 minute, three-phase, semi-structured group discussions often conducted within 12 hours of a crisis event. Defusings are designed to provide an initial forum for cathartic ventilation and information exchange.

Historically, defusings were commonly done once, then followed by a CISD. More recent mass disaster applications have seen the defusing repeated as needed during a prolonged event and commonly done more than 12 hours after the impact of a critical incident.

(5) *Critical Incident Stress Debriefing.* CISD (Mitchell, 1983; Mitchell & Everly, 2001) is a more structured, seven-phase group crisis intervention used to facilitate psychological closure and reconstruction. The CISD is a group discussion wherein participants are encouraged to discuss the critical incident and their reactions to the incident. Suggestions are provided for coping and stress management, while group member support is certainly welcomed, when appropriate. The CISD is to be used once active participation in the critical incident, disaster, or military deployment, by the participants of the CISD group, has ended. As such, it may be thought of as a "ritual of closure." Participation in the CISD is voluntary.

Historically, the CISD was typically employed one to three days post-incident and would consist of 3 to 50 individuals and last up to three hours. More recently, the CISD has been employed 1 to 14 days post-incident. In the case of mass disasters or prolonged crisis events, the CISD may be performed months after the initial impact, keeping in mind the CISD as a "ritual of closure." Thus, an important tactical alteration that has been implemented is the necessity to consider time as a psychological variable, not a temporal one. Psychological readiness for the CISD is important to consider. Another tactical alteration in the use of the CISD is to only utilize the CISD with "homogeneous" groups (see Ursano, et al., 2003). Homogeneous groups are groups which are often functional workgroups (an engine company in fire suppression, a platoon in the military, an office workgroup in business, etc.). "Debriefing of nonhomogeneous groups (e.g., greatly varied exposures) can actually increase exposure of individuals to the traumatic experiences through the storytelling of others" (Ursano, et al., 2003, p. 336). The size of the group has emerged as an important dynamic to consider. Smaller group are typically shorter in duration and may achieve greater cohesion. Lastly, although not prescribed, the CISD has sometimes been used as a "stand-alone" intervention. To reiterate a point made earlier, CISD is only one component within an integrated response system and was not designed to be used in functional isolation or as a stand-alone intervention.

(6) Family crisis intervention. Family crisis intervention refers to the provision of acute psychological support to the family units of emergency services personnel, military members, and even civilian employees subsequent to violence, disasters, and other critical incidents at work.

Historically, families were often left out of the crisis intervention response. The military has done the most to see that acute mental health services are made available to family members whether they be primary, secondary, or tertiary victims. "Spouses of disasters workers need to be educated about their loved one's experiences. Many workers claimed that they wished their spouses had been informed of the nature of their work. Information can be provided to spouses in order to allay their concerns. This will also reinforce this naturally occurring support system. Brief groups held for spouses can also be a useful intervention" (Ursano, McCarroll, & Fullerton, 2003, p. 328).

7) Individual crisis intervention. Crisis intervention with individuals, one at a time, is an essential element in the CISM approach. This form of crisis intervention is the most widely used of all crisis interventions, whether it is face-to-face or telephonic, as in a telephone hotline. This form of crisis intervention remains the most widely used form of crisis intervention and disaster response mechanism.

Historically, one-on-one crisis intervention was practiced in a virtual vacuum without recognition of the wide array of additional intervention tactics that were available (such as those enumerated on this list). For example, while potentially effective, one-on-one crisis intervention, by definition and practice, lacks the added advantages ("curative factors") of any form of group crisis intervention (see Yalom, 1970), when such is indicated. One-on-one crisis intervention may be paired with each of the other interventions on this list consonant with Millon's notion of potentiating pairings.

(8) Pastoral crisis intervention. "Pastoral crisis intervention," (Everly, 2000b, 2000c) refers to the utilization of specially trained faith-oriented personnel in the provision of acute psychological support during, or anytime after, a critical incident or mass disaster.

Historically, utilization of the faith-based community, during and after critical incidents, was often a "catch as catch can" process. Some of those called upon possessed extraordinary training and competence in crisis intervention, while

the only qualification for others was ordination. The pastoral crisis intervention movement simply mandates that those from the faith-based community who function in the field of crisis intervention and disaster response receive specialized training in emergency/disaster mental health response to critical incidents and mass disasters.

(9) Organizational consultation and development. Emergency mental health consultation and organizational development with institutional management/command staff is another important aspect of CISM. Here, the role of emergency mental health becomes assisting in strategic planning and consulting on tactical situations from a psychological perspective.

Historically, such a consultation function was seldom existent. When, indeed present, such consultation was subsumed within the overall "health" function within a given organization or community. Now, emergency mental health may be seen as a unique expertise making a valuable contribution in its own right. As a result, this function has evolved to become a potential constituent of the Emergency/Disaster Operations Center within the overall ICS. "Organizational interventions after disasters and terrorism may be very important for assisting the recovery of the community. Leaders often find consultation about the expected human responses, phases of recovery, timing of recovery, identification of high-risk groups, and the monitoring of rest, respite, and leadership stress to be helpful" (Ursano, et al., 2003, p. 335).

10) Follow-up and referral. Follow-up with individuals, groups, and even communities, subsequent to the initial crisis intervention and facilitating access to the next level of formalized medical and/psychological intervention is an absolutely essential aspect of CISM.

Historically, crisis intervention was often seen as a "one shot" intervention. Now, both strategically and tactically, emergency mental health should be viewed as one point on an integrated continuum of care (British Psychological Society, 1990; Everly & Mitchell, 1999; Professional Practice Working Group, 2002; Ursano, et al., 2003). It is this aspect which ensures the applicability of CISM and other systems' approaches (such as the American Red Cross, NOVA, and the Salvation Army) to all victims of trauma and disaster, regardless of the severity of manifest distress. Often, successful crisis intervention is defined simply by identifying those victims who require more intense intervention than acute psychological support (Ursano, et al., 2003). In emergency medicine, a successful intervention may be defined by having the emergency medical technicians simply "stabilize and transport" the medical patient, rather than achieving a "cure." Successful intervention in the field of emergency mental health may be defined as having the crisis interventionist stabilize and facilitate access to the next level of care, rather than affecting a "cure." Thus screening and triage may be considered as successful outcomes in both physical medicine as well as emergency mental health.

Evolution of Training in Early Psychological Intervention

As the perceived need for emergency/disaster mental health services grows, the need for appropriate training would appear to emerge as an important issue. Whether as part of pre-doctoral academic training, internship, or residency training, it may be that there exist "core competencies" in emergency/disaster mental health. Everly (2002) has argued that the core competencies may be thought of as follows:

1. the ability to differentiate benign vs. malignant psychological symptomatology;
2. skill in one-on-one crisis intervention (face-to-face or telephonically)
3. skill in small group crisis intervention (20 or less);
4. skill in large group crisis intervention (20 to 300); and,
5. the ability to plan and implement an integrated , phasic multi-component emergency mental health initiative residing within the confines of an overall ICS.

As one peruses the five training competencies enumerated above, it becomes clear that the ability to differentiate benign from malignant symptomatology combined with the clinical skill of working one-on-one with an individual in crisis are *the "bedrock" foundational competencies in crisis intervention and emergency/disaster mental health* as they represent not only the core content skills, but they represent the core processes undergirding all emergency psychological interventions. Skills in small group crisis intervention and large group crisis intervention are useful and important skills to possess, but in terms of frequency of utilization and the process of intervention itself, *the skills associated with providing acute individual "psychological first aid" are the virtual sine qua non* and should be the basis from which all other training evolves.

Summary

The field of emergency/disaster mental health represents an important addition to the mental health professions. Like psychotherapy, pharmacotherapy, and group therapy, it requires specialized training (Dyregrov, 1998). Unlike psychotherapy, psychopharmacotherapy, and group therapy, it is in its infancy. Since its rudimentary beginnings, it has been shown to evolve both tactically and strategically in response to expanding demands. This dynamism, it may be suggested, is a sign of a healthy system.

References

Arendt, M., & Elklit, A. (2001). Effectiveness of psychological debriefing. *Acta Psychiatrica Scandinavica*, 104, 423-437.

Artiss, K. (1963). Human behavior under stress: From combat to social psychiatry. *Military Medicine*, 128, 1011-1015.

British Psychological Society's Working Party (1990). *Psychological Aspects of Disaster*. Leicester,UK: British Psychological Society.

Deahl, M. (2000) Psychological debriefing: controversy and challenge. *Australian and New Zealand Journal of Psychiatry*, 34, 929-939.

Deahl, M., Srinivasan, M., Jones, N., Thomas, J., Neblett, C., & Jolly, A. (2000). Preventing psychological trauma in soldiers. The role of operational stress training and psychological debriefing. *British Journal of Medical Psychology*, 73, 77-85.

Deahl, M., Srinivasan, M., Jones, N., Neblett, C., & Jolly, A. (2001). Evaluating psychological debriefing: are we measuring the right outcomes? *Journal of Traumatic Stress*, 14, 527-528.

Dyregrov, A. (1998). Psychological debriefing: An effective method? *TRAUMATOLOGYe, 4*, (2), Article 1.

Everly, G.S., Jr. (1995). The role of the critical incident stress debriefing (CISD) process in disaster counseling. *Journal of Mental Health Counseling*, 17, 278-290.

Everly, G.S., Jr. (2000a). Crisis management briefings (CMB): Large group crisis intervention in response to terrorism, disasters, and violence. *International Journal of Emergency Mental Health, 2*, 53-57.

Everly, G.S., Jr. (2000b). Pastoral crisis intervention: Toward a definition. *International Journal of Emergency Mental Health, 2,* 69-71.

Everly, G.S., Jr. (2000c). The role of pastoral crisis intervention in disasters, terrorism, violence, and other community crises. *International Journal of Emergency Mental Health, 2,* 139-142.

Everly, G.S., Jr. (2002). Thoughts on training guidelines in emergency mental health and crisis intervention. *International Journal of Emergency Mental Health, 4,* 139-141.

Everly G.S., Jr., & Castellano, C. (in press). Psychological counterterrorism. *Journal of Counterterrorism and Homeland Security International.*

Everly, G.S., Jr., & Mitchell, J. (1999). *Critical Incident Stress Management (CISM): A New Era and Standard of Care in Crisis Intervention, 2nd Ed.,* Ellicott City, MD: Chevron Publishing.

Flannery, R.B., Jr. (2001). Assaulted Staff Action Program (ASAP): Ten years of empirical support for Critical Incident Stress Management (CISM). *International Journal of Emergency Mental Health, 3,* 5-10.

Flannery, R.B., Jr. (1999). Critical Incident Stress Management and the Assaulted Staff Action Program. *International Journal of Emergency Mental Health, 1,* 103-108.

Flannery, R.B., Jr., Hanson, M., Penk, W., Flannery, G., & Gallagher, C.(1995).The Assaulted Staff Action Program: An approach to coping with the aftermath of violence in the workplace. In L. Murphy, J. Hurrell, S. Sauter, and G. Keita (Eds.). *Job Stress Interventions* (pp. 199-212). Washington, D.C.: APA Press.

Flannery, R.B., Penk, W., & Corrigan, M. (1999). Assaulted Staff Action Program (ASAP) and declines in the prevalence of assaults: Community-based replication. *International Journal of Emergency Mental Health, 1,* 19-22.

Millon, T., Grossman, S., Meagher, S., Millon, C., & Everly, G. (1999). *Personality-Guided Therapy.* NY: Wiley.

Mitchell, J.T. (1983).When disaster strikes...The Critical Incident Stress Debriefing process. *Journal of Emergency Medical Services, 8,* 36-39.

Mitchell, J.T., & Everly, G. (1993). *Critical Incident Stress Debriefing: An Operations Manual (1st ed.).* Ellicott City, MD: Chevron Publishing.

Mitchell, J.T., & Everly, G. (2001). *Critical Incident Stress Debriefing: An Operations Manual (3rd ed.).* Ellicott City, MD: Chevron Publishing.

Newman, E.C. (2000). Group crisis intervention in a school setting following an attempted suicide. *International Journal of Emergency Mental Health, 2,* 97-100.

Professional Practice Board Working Party (2002). *Psychological Debriefing.* Leicester, UK: British Psychological Society.

Salmon, T.S. (1919). War neuroses and their lesson. *New York Medical Journal, 108,* 993-994.

Ursano, R., Fullerton, C., & Norwood, A. (2003). Terrorism and disasters: Prevention, intervention, and recovery. In R. Ursano, C. Fullerton, & A. Norwood (eds). *Terrorism and Disaster* (pp. 333-339). Cambridge, UK: Cambridge University Press.

Ursano, R., McCarroll, J., & Fullerton, C. (2003). Traumatic death in terrorism and disasters. In R. Ursano, C. Fullerton, & A. Norwood (eds). *Terrorism and Disaster* (pp. 308-332). Cambridge, UK: Cambridge University Press.

Yalom, I. (1970). *Group Psychotherapy.* NY: Basic.

Thoughts on Peer (Paraprofessional) Support in the Provision of Mental Health Services

George S. Everly, Jr.

ABSTRACT: *Whether providing emergency mental health services or traditional counseling, the rapid establishment of credibility and rapport represent a significant challenge for the interventionist in the development of the therapeutic relationship. The provision of "peer" psychological support represents an intuitively compelling mechanism for meeting such a challenge, especially when dealing with recipients who are unfamiliar with, or are otherwise resistant to, mental health intervention. If cautiously applied and generously supervised, the use of peer psychological support may allow the provision of psychological support services to those who might otherwise avoid such support. [International Journal of Emergency Mental Health, 2002 4(2), pp 89-90].*

KEY WORDS: peer support, peer counseling, paraprofessional counseling, crisis intervention, emergency mental health.

On February 5, 1963, with his Message on Mental Illness and Mental Retardation to the Congress of the United States, the late President John Kennedy changed the manner in which mental healthcare would be provided. This address heralded the creation of a national community mental health system predicated upon the principles of prevention and outreach. An outgrowth of the community mental health movement was the establishment of crisis intervention hotlines and walk-in psychological clinics. Many of these facilities were staffed in part by volunteers, drawn from their respective communities, who did not possess professional degrees in mental health. They were referred to as paraprofessional, or "peer," counselors. In the present context, the term "peer" counselor/ interventionist shall refer to any person, drawn from any unique geographic, educational, occupational, religious, or cultural "community," who is engaged in the provision of mental health support, but does not possess a professional degree in mental health services.

Not only were peer counselors seen as capable of functionally expanding the mental health center's ability to

George S. Everly Jr, Ph.D., F.A.P.M., International Critical Incident Stress Foundation, Loyola College in Maryland, The Union Memorial Hospital. Address correspondence concerning this article to: Dr. George Everly, Jr., 702 Severnside Ave. Severna Park, MD 21146.

provide services, but the utilization of peer counselors was also seen as a means of enhancing the effectiveness of community outreach. This by virtue of the inherent credibility (ethos) possessed by the community peers compared to the view which the denizens of the community might have of mental health professionals as too academic or "removed" from the realities of daily life. Indeed, credibility and rapport are acknowledged as essential elements in virtually all variations within the art of psychological support (see Frank & Frank, 1991; Everly, 2001).

When Peers Are Most Effective

There does not seem to be a general consensus on precisely when the use of peer (paraprofessional) counselors is most effective. Nevertheless, the following guidelines may be of value. Consider using supervised peer counseling as one aspect within the overall mental health delivery system whenever the group targeted for mental health services:

1. is uniquely educated, compared to the general population;
2. possesses highly unique occupational training (e.g., medicine, nursing, law enforcement, fire suppression, commercial airline industry, military);

3. is resistant to, or threatened by, the notion of mental health services;

4. possesses some religious or cultural characteristic which would complicate the provision of traditional mental health services; and/ or

5. believes it is not understood, or is misunderstood, by the general population outside of itself, and/ or the traditional mental health community.

The Issue of Effectiveness

Clearly, the use of peer counselors may be efficient if it expands the availability of competent mental health resources, even though they require professional oversight and ongoing supervision. But can such paraprofessional mental health resources be clinically effective?

In their classic treatise on effective counseling and psychotherapy, Truax and Carkhuff (1967) provide compelling evidence that the presence of three psychotherapeutic ingredients, specifically: 1) accurate empathy, 2) nonpossessive warmth, and 3) genuineness in and of themselves serve to support psychological well-being. They provide evidence that paraprofessionals can be taught to provide these ingredients. They conclude, "The current available evidence, then, suggests that these ingredients of accurate empathy, nonpossessive warmth and therapist genuineness are "teachable"; and even nonprofessional persons lacking expert knowledge of psychopathology and personality dynamics can, under supervision, produce positive changes…" (p. 111).

Similarly, Durlak (1979) has stated, "Evaluations of research involving paraprofessional therapists have been highly positive" (p.80). There is evidence that groups as diverse as college students, parents, and community volunteers can be effective in providing psychological support.

In a statistical review using Glass's meta-analytic formula corrected by gamma function, Hattie, Sharpley, & Rogers (1984) reviewed 154 comparisons extracted from 39 investigations. They concluded, "There does appear to be substantial evidence that paraprofessionals should be considered as effective additions to the helping services…" (p. 534).

Summary

Regarding the provision of mental health services, one of most significant challenges is the rapid establishment of trust, credibility, and general communicative rapport. In many ways, this is the sine qua non of the therapeutic relationship; and it may be that the therapeutic relationship is the sine qua non of positive therapeutic outcome. This conjecture may possess even greater relevance to the provision of emergency mental health services (crisis intervention) where time is often of the essence. Any strategic or tactical approach which facilitates the formation of the therapeutic alliance, without dangerously compromising clinical outcome, warrants serious consideration for inclusion in the overall therapeutic armamentarium. From both the intuitive, as well as the empirical perspectives, peer (paraprofessional) support warrants consideration within a myriad of mental health delivery systems. However, it seems that those selected to provide such peer support must receive 1) specialized training in crisis intervention (40 to 100 hours of training as a minimum range), and 2) adequate ongoing professional mental health oversight and clinical supervision so as to increase the likelihood of positive outcome and to reduce the risk of iatrogenic or other sources of negative outcome.

References

Durlak, J. A. (1979). Comparative effectiveness of paraprofessional and professional helpers. *Psychological Bulletin, 86*, 80-92.

Everly, G. S., Jr. (2001).Personologic alignment and the treatment of posttraumatic distress. *International Journal of Emergency Mental Health, 3*, 171-177.

Frank, J.D. & Frank, J.B. (1991). *Persuasion and Healing*, 3rd

Edition. Baltimore: Johns Hopkins University Press.

Hattie, J. A., Sharpley, C., & Rogers, H.J. (1984). Comparative effectiveness of professional and paraprofessional helpers. *Psychological Bulletin, 95*, 534-541.

Truax, C. B. & Carkhuff, R. (1967). Toward effective counseling and psychotherapy. Chicago: Aldine.

Editorial

Toward a Model of Psychological Triage: Who Will Most Need Assistance?

George S. Everly. Jr., Ph.D., F.A.P.M.

ABSTRACT: *While well developed within physical medicine, the concept of triage within emergency mental health is ill-defined. The purpose of this paper is to offer one formulation and a rudimentary set of guidelines for the process of psychological triage for individuals in crisis. These recommendations are unique in that they reflect an integration of clinical empiricism and applied physiological concepts. It is hoped that such an initiative will assist in the most efficient and effective allocation of mental health resources in acute crises, traumas, disasters, and even combat-related situations. [International Journal of Emergency Mental Health, 1999, 3, 151-154.]*

KEY WORDS: psychological triage; emergency mental health; disaster mental health; trauma; triage; crisis intervention

The term triage finds its origins in the French language and means to pick, or select. Within the context of healthcare, the term triage refers to a qualitative selection process based upon the severity of a wound or illness, coupled with the overall suitability for treatment, or intervention.

Within the domain of emergency medicine, functional guidelines and protocols for triage are relatively well established. Within the domain of emergency mental health, however, such standardized clinical protocols are conspicuous in their absence. The protocols that do exist, are not readily supported by principles of applied science. The purpose of this paper is to offer one formulation and rudimentary set of guidelines for the process of psychological triage for individuals in crisis. These recommendations may not necessarily apply when considering the selection of group crisis intervention techniques such as Critical Incident Stress Debriefings (CISD), defusings, and demobilization techniques, (see Everly and Mitchell, 1999 for a discussion of these techniques) for such interventions may actually be used as a forum, or venue, for the triage process itself. The extant recommendations are unique in that they reflect an integration of clinically-oriented empiricism and applied physiological concepts as they apply to the triage process for any given individual.

George S. Everly, Jr., Ph.D., Loyola College in Maryland and The Johns Hopkins University. Address correspondence concerning this article to: George S. Everly, Jr., Ph.D., 702 Severnside Ave., Severna Park, MD 21146

Intervention Guidelines

In physical medicine, it is typically easier to assess the need for treatment when compared to the domain of mental health. Intervention is based upon the observation of physical signs of injury and/or the report of symptoms.

In emergency mental health, or crisis intervention, signs and symptoms are less readily accessible and their meanings are less discernable to the crisis interventionist. Often the provision of crisis intervention services within the domain of emergency mental health is predicated upon the nature of an observable crisis event, despite the absence of signs or symptoms indicative of decompensation or significant distress. It is certainly important to mobilize emergency mental health resources based upon the nature of a crisis event. Nevertheless, the actual operational implementation, or engagement, of those resources, when considering individual crisis intervention (one-on-one intervention), should typically be in response to a demonstrated need, i.e., some evidence that the individual is suffering from significant distress, dysfunction, or impairment (see Everly and Mitchell, 1999). To reiterate, this concept appears most relevant when assisting individual persons in crisis as opposed to the implementation of group crisis intervention services (Everly and Mitchell, 1999). Indeed, criticisms have recently emerged in the popular media suggesting that the mental health professions routinely "over respond" to crisis and disaster events. In doing so, it has been suggested that emergency mental health services may actually serve as obstacles to natural recovery processes if applied too early, and may further create a condition of iatrogenic victimization. It is beyond the scope of this paper to debate the latter contention, rather it seems more useful to offer a review of core principles and recommendations regarding individual psychological triage, that may be of assistance in sharpening the focus of emergency mental health interventions when applied to individuals in crisis.

Let us begin with the notion of a psychological crisis. A crisis may be thought of as an acute response exhibited by an individual wherein:

1. psychological homeostasis has been disrupted;
2. one's usual coping mechanisms have failed in their efforts to either solve the problem, or otherwise reestablish psychological homeostasis; and,
3. the distress engendered by the crisis has yielded some evidence of functional impairment (Everly, 1999).

By honing in on the salient signs and symptoms of distress, the crisis interventionist increases the likelihood that psychological support services will be provided to those who most need them, while at the same time not "over responding," i.e., providing interventions to those who don't need the services, while also avoiding the practice of psychotherapy. It should also be noted that in many instances, the situations that require the most intense psychological interventions will be situations that require complex physical search, rescue, and recovery interventions. Such situations include mass shootings, airplane disasters, bombings, earthquakes, hurricanes and the like. It therefore becomes possible for the psychological crisis interventionists to inadvertently become intrusive to the operational aspects of disaster intervention.

What then are the most common signs and symptoms that serve to predict poor mental health outcomes if no intervention is provided? What are the signs and symptoms of individual distress that should be used as the basis for decision making in the process of psychologcial triage? What are the signs and symptoms that would serve to best denote who will most need support in a crisis? The following guidelines for psychological triage are based upon, not only a review of the extant literature, but also upon reflection of Walter Cannon's "wisdom of the body" (Cannon, 1932).

Cannon's formulations allow us to anticipate which reactions to crisis and traumatic events are constructive, psychophysiologically speaking, and which reactions may portend a poor mental health prognosis. Simple, concise, yet penetrating in its implications, Cannon's (1932) formulation

of the "fight or flight" response can serve as a useful guide directing one's efforts in psychological triage. Simply stated, the manifest psychophysiology that characterizes the adaptive crisis response is one that prepares the person to survive. Indeed, the "fight or flight" response is a survival mechanism, i.e., mobilization of these psychophysiological mechanisms actually serve to enhance the likelihood of physical survival in the face of a life-threatening challenge. The mechanisms undergirding an adaptive response to a crisis or traumatic situation would be:

1. enhanced activation of the sympathetic branch of the autonomic nervous system;
2. enhanced activity of the neuromuscular system; and,
3. enhanced activation of the sympatho-adrenal medullary system (see Everly, 1989 for a complete discussion of these mechanisms).

Thus, based upon the conceptualization of Cannon, one would expect that symptoms of stress, experienced during a crisis, that may be seen as consonant with the survival aspects of the aforementioned "fight or flight" response (and its undergirding mechanisms) are less likely to predict poor mental health outcome such as posttraumatic stress disorder. Acute episodes of muscle aches, tachycardia, cold hands and feet, elevations in blood pressure, hyperstartle response, hypervigilance, mild agitation, forcused aggressiveness, diminished appetite, diminished gastrointestinal motility, diminished libido, etc., while disconcerting, tend to be short-lived and do not portend poor mental health outcome. See Everly (1989) for a more complete listing of adaptive manifestations of the human stress response.

Conversely, signs and symptoms that are in juxtaposition to Cannon's formulations of the "fight or flight" survival mechanism would be expected to predict poorer psychological outcome, if no crisis intervention services are provided. The mechanisms undergirding a counter productive response to a crisis situation would be:

1. enhanced activation of the parasympathetic branch of the autonomic nervous system;
2. dysfunctional over-excitation of the sympathetic nervous system;
3. dysfunctional over-excitation of the sympatho-adrenal medullary system;
4. neuromuscular immobility; and/or,
5. cognitive impairments that would impair adaptive responding to the perceived threat.

Thus, signs and symptoms that would be consistent with the aforementioned mechanisms, which would suggest a poorer mental health outcome, and which would serve as indicative of a greater potential need for psychological support might include the following acute, peritraumatic or chronic manifestations:

1. neuromuscular "freezing" (Levine, 1997; Lee, Vaillant, Torrey, & Elder, 1995),
2. severe time distortion (Fontana & Rosenheck, 1993),
3. psychogenic analgesia (Fontana & Rosenheck, 1993),
4. traumatic psychogenic amnesia (Fontana & Rosenheck, 1993),
5. dissociation, depersonalization and/or derealization (Marmar, Weiss, Schlenger, et al., 1994; Weiss, Marmar, Metzler, & Ronfeldt, 1995; Koopman, Classen, & Spiegal, 1994; Holen, 1993; Shalev, et al., 1996),
6. manifestations of sympathetic nervous system dysfunction (Everly, 1989; Brewin, Andrews, Rose, & Kirk, 1999),
7. manifestations of enhanced parasympathetic arousal (Everly, 1989; Lee, Vaillant, Torrey, & Elder, 1995),
8. guilt reactions, including "survivor guilt" (Holen, 1993; see Peterson, Prout, & Schwarz, 1991),
9. helpless, hopeless ideation (Seligman, 1975), and
10. suicidal and/or homicidal ideation.

These, then, constitute the signs and symptoms of acute distress that most warrant individual crisis intervention.

Conclusion

Psychological triage with individual persons in crisis is the embodiment of the notion that not all participants in crisis and disaster events require emergency mental health care. Indeed, for some, intervention may be construed as interference with the natural recovery mechanisms. Similarly, during times of limited intervention resources, there is a need to identify those persons in most need of care. Individual, one-on-one crisis intervention services should be prioritized for those who most require and can benefit from such services. The operationalization of psychological triage is selecting who will receive intervention and who will not. This paper offers guidelines for the determination of who will most need individual crisis intervention (individual one-on-one intervention) subsequent to a traumatic event, or critical incident, based upon the observation of signs and symptoms that are in juxtaposition to Cannon's formulation of the constructive use of the "fight of flight" response. It may be argued that such manifestations predict poor mental health outcome because they represent contradictions to the "wisdom of the body." That is, they serve to interfere with the quest for physical survival (see Table 1 below). These guidelines may not be useful for the implementation of group crisis intervention services, such as the CISD however, since such interventions may actually be used as a triage forum and may then be implemented based upon the nature of the crisis event. In the final analysis, by focusing on the most salient signs and symptoms of distress, emergency mental health services are more likely to be provided to those who most need them, while at the same time not wasting resources and not "over responding."

Table 1: Peritraumatic Predictors and Warning Signs of Posttraumatic Distress

1. Neuromuscular immobility, "freezing"
2. Severe dysfunctional time distortion
3. Psychogenic analgesia
4. Traumatic psychogenic amnesia
5. Dissociation, depersonalization, derealization
6. Sympathetic nervous system dysfunction, e.g. panic attacks, malignant arrhythmias
7. Dysfunctional parasympathetic nervous system arousal
8. Guilt reactions (survivor guilt, responsibility guilt)
9. "Giving up," e.g., helplessness, hopelessness
10. Self-destructive ideation, e.g., suicidal and/or homicidal ideation.

References

Brewin, C., Andrews, B., Rose, S., & Kirk, M. (1999). Acute stress disorder and posttraumatic stress disorder in victims of violent crime. *American Journal of Psychiatry, 156,* 360-366.

Cannon, W. (1932). *The wisdom of the body.* NY: Norton.

Everly, G.S. (1999). A primer on Critical Incident Stress Management: What's really in a name? *International Journal of Emergency Mental Health, 1,* 77-80. Ellicott City, MD: Chevron Publishing Corporation.

Everly, G.S. (1989). *A clinical guide to the treatment of the human stress response.* NY: Plenum.

Everly, G.S. & Mitchell, J.T. (1999). *Critical Incident Stress Management (CISM): A new era and standard of care in crisis intervention.* Ellicott City, MD: Chevron Publishing Corporation.

Fontana, A. & Rosenheck, R. (1993). A causal model of the etiology of war-related PTSD. *Journal of Traumatic Stress, 6,* 475-500.

Holen, A. (1993). *The North Sea oil rig disaster.* In J. Wilson and B. Raphael (Eds.). *International Handbook of Traumatic Stress Symdroms,* (pp. 471-478). NY: Plenum.

Koopman, C., Classen, C., & Spiegel, D. (1994). Predictors of posttraumatic stress symptoms among survivors of the Oakland / Berkeley, California firestorm. *American Journal of Psychiatry, 151,* 888-894.

Lee, K.A., Vaillant, G., Torrey, W., & Elder, G. (1995). A 50 year prospective study of the psychological sequelae of World War II combat. *American Journal of Psychiatry, 152,* 516-522.

Levine, P. (1997). *Waking the Tiger.* Berkeley, CA: North Atlantic Books.

Marmar, C.R., Weiss, D., Schlenger, W., Fairbank, J., Jordan, B., Kulka, R., & Hough, R. (1994). Peritraumatic dissociation and posttraumatic stress in male Vietnam theater veterans. *American Journal of Psychiatry, 151,* 902-907.

Peterson, K., Prout, M., & Schwarz, R. (1991). *Post-Traumatic Stress Disorder.* NY: Plenum.

Seligman, M.E.P. (1975). *Helplessness: On depression, development, and death.* San Fransisco: Freeman.

Shalev, A.Y., Peri, T., Canetti, L., & Schreiber, S. (1996). Predictors of PTSD in injured trauma survivors: A prospective study. *American Journal of Psychiatry, 153,* 219-225.

Early Psychological Intervention: A Word of Caution

George S. Everly, Jr.

ABSTRACT: *The second Gulf War and liberation of Iraq have spawned new fears of domestic terrorism. There have been numerous calls for the integration of disaster mental health services into extant public health and national defense policies (Holloway, Norwood, Fullerton, Engel & Ursano, 1997; DiGiovanni, 1999; Susser, Herman, & Aaron, 2002, August). While most agree that such a strategy is warranted, questions abound as to how the tactical components should be implemented. Furthermore, concern has been raised regarding the importance of "doing no harm" (NIMH, 2002), i.e., the risk of iatrogenic harm. This article, while acknowledging the potential value of early psychological intervention, acknowledges the potential risks associated with the form of emergency mental health intervention, often referred to as crisis intervention. The article also provides suggestions for reducing the risks for iatrogenic harm associated with crisis intervention.*

KEY WORDS: *Early psychological intervention, crisis intervention, iatrogenic harm, debriefing.*

Background

As the "war on terrorism" progresses, as military personnel engage in combat in foreign theaters, as the images of September 11, 2001, remain vivid for many, and as concern is raised over domestic preparedness in light of terrorist threats, great interest has become focused upon early psychological intervention, often referred to as crisis intervention (Caplan, 1964), psychological first aid, emergency mental health, or emotional first aid (Neil, Oney, DiFonso, Thacker, & Reichart, 1974). Conceptually, a parallel may be drawn between physical health and mental health such that "as physical first aid is to surgery, crisis intervention is to psychotherapy." As the goals of physical first aid are:

1) stabilization of physiological functioning,
2) mitigation of physiological dysfunction/distress,
3) return of acute adaptive physiological functioning, and/or
4) facilitation of access to the next level of care.

George S. Everly, Jr., Ph.D., The Johns Hopkins University, Bloomberg School of Public Health; Loyola College in Maryland; and the International Critical Incident Stress Foundation. Address correspondence concerning this article to: George Everly, Jr., 702 Severnside Ave., Severna Park, MD 21146 USA.

The goals of crisis intervention are:

1) stabilization of psychological functioning through meeting basic physical needs, then addressing the most basic of psychological needs,
2) mitigation of psychological dysfunction/distress,
3) return of acute adaptive psychological functioning, and/or
4) facilitation of access to the next level of care.

In the formative years of crisis intervention, Rapoport (1965) noted, "A little help, rationally directed and purposely focused at a strategic time is more effective than extensive help given at a period of less emotional accessibility" (p. 30). Later, Swanson and Carbon (1989) writing for the American Psychiatric Association Task Force Report on the Treatment of Psychiatric Disorders stated, "Crisis intervention is a proven approach to helping in the pain of an emotional crisis" (p. 2520).

The aforementioned assertions were made not based upon case study and field empiricism alone, but also upon well-controlled clinical investigations. Langsley, Machotka, and Flomenhaft (1971) used random assignment (RCT) of 300 patients to inpatient treatment vs. family crisis intervention. Results indicated crisis intervention was superior to inpatient treatment for preventing subsequent psychiatric hospitalizations. Decker and Stubblebine (1972) followed 540 psychiatric patients for 2.5 years subsequent to an initial psychiatric hospitalization. Traditional follow-up treatment was compared to crisis intervention services. Results supported the superiority of the crisis intervention services in preventing subsequent hospitalizations. Bunn and Clarke (1979), in a randomized controlled design with 30 individuals who had accompanied relatives to the hospital after a serious injury, found 20 minutes of supportive crisis counseling superior to no intervention in reducing anxiety. Bordow and Porritt (1979) employed a three-group RCT of individual crisis intervention with hospitalized motor vehicle accident victims. Results were indicative of a dose response relationship between intervention level and the reduction of reported distress. When crisis intervention principles and practices were applied to victims of bank robberies, the crisis interventions were found to be effective in reducing distress (Campfield & Hills, 2001; Richards, 2001). In military applications, Solomon and Benbenishty (1986) found the core crisis intervention principles of "proximity, immediacy, and expectancy" to be effective in response to combat; this consistent with the seminal observations of Salmon (1919) and Artiss (1963). Deahl, et al., (2000) found small group crisis intervention to be effective in reducing alcohol use in military personnel after returning from peace-keeping activities in a war zone. Flannery (Flannery, 2001; Flannery, Hanson & Penk, 1994; Flannery, Hanson, Penk, Flannery & Gallagher, 1995) pioneered the development of a multi-component critical incident stress management program referred to as the Assaulted Staff Action Program (ASAP). ASAP was chosen as one of the 10 best programs in 1996 by the American Psychiatric Association. A 10-year review of ASAP practice revealed ASAP to be clinically effective (Flannery, 2001). Everly, Flannery, and Mitchell (2000) performed a qualitative review of multi-component crisis intervention programs and found evidence of clinical utility.

Recently, the endeavor of providing early psychological intervention has been re-examined. Some have even called for an end to early intervention due to concern over potential iatrogenic harm as a result of crisis intervention, especially the ill-defined "psychological debriefing." Indeed, the term "debriefing" albeit poorly defined to the point of having lost any valuable denotative quality (NIMH, 2002), has come to inappropriately symbolize virtually all early psychological intervention. It now serves as a veritable "lightning rod" for the debate on early psychological interven-

tion. Nevertheless, concern over possible harm resulting from crisis intervention is a valid concern. *Clearly, however, in light of research suggesting that crisis intervention can exert positive effects, efforts should be directed toward identifying mechanisms of therapeutic effect, potential sources of adverse iatrogenesis, and compensatory strategies developed to respond to the latter.* It would seem that such is a superior course as opposed to adopting reductionistic binary thinking wherein we view, and therefore subsequently judge, crisis intervention to be "all good" or "all bad." It seems that we would want to avoid a condition wherein we "throw the baby out with the bathwater."

Psychotherapy Can Be Harmful To Your Health

The field of psychotherapy preceded the formal development of the field of crisis intervention. There may be some useful lessons therein. As the field of psychotherapy developed, it should be noted that concern was expressed regarding potential adverse iatrogenesis. Indeed, subsequent research revealed that while many patients are helped by psychotherapy, some are not, and some are even harmed by participation in psychotherapy.

There can be little disagreement with the assertion that psychotherapy can lead to negative outcomes. More specifically, Smith, Glass, and Miller (1980) in their meta-analytic review of over 400 psychotherapy outcome studies found that about 9% of the reported effect was negative. Shapiro and Shapiro (1982) in an analysis of over 1800 effect sizes found that 11% were negative and 30% were null! Mohr (1995) compiled a review of over 40 psychotherapy investigations all of which identified deterioration as a result of psychotherapy. Lambert (2003), in his most recent analysis of psychotherapy effectiveness, states, "Despite the overall positive findings, a portion of patients who enter treatment are worse off when they leave treatment than when they entered" (p. 4). He estimates that about 5 to 10% of patients "deteriorate during treatment," while another 15 to 25% show no measured benefit (Lambert, 2003). The notion of negative outcome as a result of psychotherapy is not a new revelation as Strupp, Hadley, and Gomes-Schwartz (1977), in their text *Psychotherapy for Better or Worse*, listed over 40 studies from 1950 to 1972 alone that reported negative outcome. Finally, data exist indicating that up to 29% of cognitive behavioral therapy (CBT) participants drop out of the clinical investigations (McNally, Bryant, & Ehlers, 2003), presumably due in part to distress engendered by the treatment process itself. This is especially relevant as CBT has been suggested as a possible alternative to crisis intervention. However, the CBT exposure component may be contraindicated with: extreme anxiety and panic, marked dissociation, psychosis, severe depression, suicidal risk, homicidal risk, anger, unresolved prior trauma, ongoing stressors, and acute bereavement (see Bryant & Harvey, 2000, pp. 145-146), the very presentations that an interventionist may face when doing acute crisis intervention.

The field of traditional psychotherapy is not the only mental health intervention that possesses the potential for iatrogenic adversity. In their text *Helping the Helpers Not to Harm: Iatrogenic Damage and Community Mental Health,* Caplan & Caplan (2001) skillfully point out the risks associated with community mental health initiatives.

Concerns About Early Intervention ("Debriefing")

Initial concern over the effectiveness of crisis intervention "debriefings" arose in the relevant literature with the publication of two Australian studies. McFarlane (1988) reported on the longitudinal course of posttraumatic morbidity in the wake of bush fires. One aspect of the study found that acute posttraumatic stress was predicted by avoidance of thinking about problems, property loss, and a failure to attend undefined forms of psychological debriefings. However, chronic variations of posttraumatic stress disorder were best predicted by premorbid, non-event related factors, such as a family history of psychiatric disorders, concurrent avoidance and neuroticism, and a tendency not to confront conflicts. More specifically, a delayed distress group, that received undefined "debriefings" later suffered higher levels of posttraumatic distress, however, they also had higher premorbid neuroticism scores, and greater property loss. These factors were causally and inextricably intertwined with the adverse outcome, nevertheless attribution of the adverse outcome has sometimes been inferred to have singularly arisen from the unspecified "debriefings." The second of the early negative outcome studies was that of Kenardy, et al., (1996). Kenardy's investigation purported to assess the effectiveness of stress debriefings for 62 "debriefed helpers" compared to 133 who were apparently not debriefed subsequent to an earthquake in New Castle, Australia. This study is often cited as evidence for the ineffectiveness of crisis intervention debriefings. Indeed, the "debriefed" group had more severe traumatic stress scores at 13 months, yet to their credit, the authors state, "we were not able to influence the availability or nature of the debriefing..." (p. 39). They continue, "It was assumed that all subjects in this study who reported having been debriefed did in fact receive posttrauma debriefing. However, there was no standardization of debriefing services..."(p.47). It should be of interest to note that in fact, neither Mitchell's small group crisis intervention known as Critical Incident Stress Debriefing (CISD), nor Dyregrov's small group crisis intervention Psychological Debriefing (PD), had been taught to frontline rescuers in Australia at the time of either of these studies (R. Robinson, 2002, personal communication).

The aforementioned studies aside, the primary scientific foundation for the recent criticisms of early crisis intervention, especially "debriefing," can be found in the Cochrane Library's Cochrane Reviews. Citing as evidence the results of the Cochrane Library Review of RCTs (Wessely, Rose, & Bisson, 1998; Rose, Bisson, & Wessely, 2002) and selected derivative reviews (Litz, Gray, Bryant & Adler, 2002; van Emmerick, Kamphuis, Hulsbosch & Emmelkamp, 2002), some have reached the conclusion that early psychological intervention (especially "debriefing") is ineffectual, and may cause harm to some. A few individuals have even suggested that early intervention after disasters and mass violence should be discontinued in deference to waiting 30 days posttrauma and prescribing 4 to 12 sessions of cognitive behavioral therapy (CBT).

Such conclusions based upon the Cochrane Review, its derivatives, or selected combinations of constituent studies may not be warranted, however. In point of fact, most of the constituency of Cochrane investigations represent "single session counseling with medical patients" and are in no way consistent with the principles, nor the practice, of crisis intervention in community or mass disaster settings. As such, they fail to serve as a valid comparison group from which generalizations may be made to survivors of mass disasters or even emergency services personnel. Thus, those calling for the cessation of early intervention and who use the Cochrane Review as the basis for their recommendation have extrapolated beyond the recommendations of even the Cochran authors themselves. The authors of the Cochrane Review of psychological debriefing themselves (Rose, Bisson, & Wessely, 2002), although calling for a cessation of "compulsory debriefings pending further evidence" (p. 10) have concluded, *We are unable to comment on the use of group debriefing, nor the use of debriefing after mass traumas" (p.10).*

Crisis Intervention: A Cautionary Note

Although the early Australian studies and the Cochrane Reviews may not have direct applicability to crisis intervention as it is practiced in a small group format (e.g., the Critical Incident Stress Debriefing), nor as it is practiced in response to mass disasters or community violence, as with psychotherapy, there is clearly the potential to do harm.

A review of relevant literature reveals potential "risk factors" of significance associated with crisis intervention. Those risk factors are listed below with suggestions for mitigating those risks.

1. It is imperative that emergent intervention follow the basic principles and hierarchy of needs, i.e., meeting basic needs first. More specifically, needs for food, water, shelter, alleviation of pain, reunification with family members, and the provision of a sense of safety and security should all precede the utilization of psychologically-oriented crisis interventions.

2. As compulsory participation in crisis intervention is likely to be perceived negatively, participation in any psychologically-oriented crisis intervention activities should be voluntary accompanied by some form of relevant informed consent when intervention goes beyond simple information or educational briefings.

3. Group crisis intervention poses a risk for iatrogenic harm if it introduces traumatogenetic material to group members who would not otherwise be exposed to such material. To reduce this risk, it is suggested that small crisis intervention groups be made up of naturally occurring cohorts and/or homogeneous groups with regard to trauma exposure and toxicity. The formation of small heterogeneous crisis intervention debriefings should not be endorsed.

4. It has been proposed that health education about signs and symptoms of distress may actually psychogenically create such symptoms in highly suggestible persons. It is hard to accept this notion of potential mass hysteria so as to "keep information from people for their own good." Nevertheless, it may be argued that the manner in which the information is presented may have a significant effect upon subsequent hysterical symptomatology. Such information should be presented as basic health education related information designed to empower the recipients of such information to assume more, not less, control in responding to adversity, when such seems appropriate.

5. The notion of the value of cathartic ventilation has been challenged to the degree that concern has been expressed that cathartic ventilation may become a pathogenic abreactive process. To reduce this risk, it might be suggested that assessment and triage are essential elements of effective crisis intervention wherein psychologically vulnerable or brittle persons (highly aroused, morbidly depressed, highly guilt-ridden individuals, the intensely bereaved, dissociating individuals, those experiencing psychotic symptomatology, those physically injured or in pain) not be included in group crisis intervention, rather, they should be approached individually and more appropriate interventions should be utilized. Furthermore, whether individually or in groups, deep probing techniques, psychotherapeutic interpretation, and paradoxical intention should clearly be avoided.

6. Concern has been expressed that crisis intervention techniques should never consist of univariate standalone interventions. Rather, crisis intervention should consist of a phase sensitive, multi-variate intervention system. Consistent with the notion of integrative psychotherapy, crisis intervention should be integrative, i.e., crisis intervention should be conceived of as a configurational system of strategies and tactics in which each intervention technique is selected not only for its efficacy in resolving singular clinical and pre-clinical features but also for its contribution to the overall constellation of intervention procedures in their task of responding to the unique demands of any given circumstance (adapted from Millon, 2003).

7. So that crisis intervention is not conceived of as a substitute for more formal psychotherapeutic and/or psychiatric interventions, crisis intervention is conceived of as but one point on a continuum of care which certainly includes psychotherapy. The natural corollary of this conceptualization is that successful crisis intervention, similar to successful physical first aid, may actually consist of simply facilitating access to the next and more appropriate level of care.

8. Lastly, it is essential that those practicing psychological crisis intervention receive specialized training to do so (Dyregrov, 1999). Standard counseling and psychotherapy training will typically prove inadequate to respond effectively to mass disasters, large-scale violence, terrorism, and even well circumscribed acute crises.

Summary

This article has attempted to sensitize the reader and provide a cautionary note as to the risks associated with psychological crisis intervention. As a prerequisite to doing so, however, it was essential to point out the facts that the risks associated with crisis intervention, "debriefing," and disaster mental health are not unique.

Clearly, there are risks associated with any endeavor that attempts to assist those who are physically and/or psychologically distressed. There are risks associated with the consumption of aspirin.

Of greater relevance, however, there is value in pointing out that the practice of psychotherapy is replete with risks of null outcome as well as iatrogenic harm. While there have been calls for the cessation of crisis intervention because of perceived risk, there have been no calls for the cessation of psychotherapy even though the documented risks of psychotherapy are far greater.

To reiterate an earlier point, in light of research suggesting that crisis intervention can exert positive effects, efforts should be directed toward identifying mechanisms of therapeutic effect, identifying potential sources of adverse iatrogenesis, and identifying compensatory strategies that be employed to reduce the risk of iatrogenic harm. It would seem that such a tact is clearly a superior course as opposed to adopting binary thinking wherein we view, and therefore subsequently judge, crisis intervention to be "all good" or "all bad." It seems that we would want to avoid a condition wherein we "throw the baby out with the bathwater."

References

Artiss, K. (1963). Human behavior under stress: From combat to social psychiatry. *Military Medicine*, 128, 1011-1015.

Bordow, S., & Porritt, D. (1979). An experimental evaluation of crisis intervention. *Social Science and Medicine*, 13, 251-256.

Bryant, R., & Harvey, A.G. (2000). Acute stress disorder. Wash., D.C.: American Psychological Association Press.

Bunn, T., & Clarke, A. (1979). Crisis intervention. *British Journal of Medical Psychology*, 52, 191-195.

Campfield, K., & Hills, A. (2001). Effect of timing of critical Incident Stress Debriefing (CISD) on posttraumatic symptoms. *Journal of Traumatic Stress*, 14, 327-340.

Caplan, G. (1964). *Principles of preventive psychiatry*. NY: Basic Books.

Caplan, R., & Caplan, G. (2001). *Helping the helpers not to harm*. NY: Brunner.

Deahl, M., Srinivasan, M., Jones, N., Thomas, J., Neblett, C., & Jolly, A. (2000). Preventing psychological trauma in soldiers. The role of operational stress training and psychological debriefing. *British Journal of Medical Psychology*, 73, 77-85.

Decker, J., & Stubblebine, J. (1972). Crisis intervention and prevention of psychiatric disability: A follow-up. *American Journal of Psychiatry*, 129, 725-729.

DiGiovanni, C. (1999). Domestic terrorism with chemical or biological agents: Psychiatric aspects. *American Journal of Psychiatry*, 156, 1500-1505.

Dyregrov, A. (1999). Helpful and hurtful aspects of psychological debriefing groups. *International Journal of Emergency Mental Health*, 3, 175-182.

Everly, G.S., Flannery, R.B., & Mitchell, J. (2000). Critical incident stress management: A review of the literature. *Aggression and Violent Behavior*, 5, 23-40.

Flannery, R.B. (2001). Assaulted Staff Action Program (ASAP): Ten years of empirical support for Critical Incident Stress Management (CISM). *International Journal of Emergency Mental Health*, 3, 5-10.

Flannery, R.B., Hanson, M., & Penk, W. (1994). Risk factors for psychiatric inpatient assaults on staff. *The Journal of Mental Health Administration*, 21, 24-31.

Flannery, R.B., Hanson, M., Penk, W., Flannery, G., & Gallagher, C.(1995).The Assaulted Staff Action Program: An approach to coping with the aftermath of violence in the workplace. In L. Murphy, J. Hurrell, S. Sauter, and G. Keita (Eds.). *Job Stress Interventions* (pp. 199-212). Washington, D.C.: APA Press.

Holloway, H., Norwood, A., Fullerton, C., Engel, C., & Ursano, R. (1967). The threat of biological weapons. *Journal of the American Medical Association*, 278, 425-427.

Kenardy, J.A., Webster, R.A., Lewin, T.J., Carr, V.J., Hazell, P.L., & Carter, G.L. (1996) Stress debriefing and patterns of recovery following a natural disaster. *Journal of Traumatic Stress*, 9, 37-49.

Langsley, D., Machotka, P., & Flomenhaft, K. (1971). Avoiding mental health admission: A follow-up. *American Journal of Psychiatry*, 127, 1391-1394.

Lambert, M. J. (2003). The effectiveness of psychotherapy: What has a century of research taught us about the effects of treatment. Psychotherapeutically Speaking— Updates from the Division of Psychotherapy. Washington, D.C.: American Psychological Association.

Litz, B., Gray, M., Bryant, R., & Adler, A. (2002). Early intervention for trauma: Current status and future directions. *Clinical Psychology Science and Practice, 9,* 112-134.

McFarlane, A.C. (1988). The longitudinal course of post-traumatic morbidity. *Journal of Nervous and Mental Disease, 176,* 30-39.

McNally, R., Bryant, R., & Ehlers, A. (2003) Does early psychological intervention promote recovery from post-traumatic stress? *Psychological Science in the Public Interest, 4,* 45-79.

Millon, T. (2003). It's time to rework the blueprints: Building a science for clinical psychology. American Psychologist, 58, 949-960.

Mohr, D. C. (1995). Negative outcome in psychotherapy: A critical review. *Clinical Psychology: Science and Practice, 2,* 1-27.

National Institute of Mental Health (2002). *Mental Health and Mass Violence.* Washington, D.C.: Author.

Neil, T. C., Oney, J.E., DiFonso, L., Thacker, B., & Reichart, W. (1974). *Emotional first aid.* Louisville, KY: Kemper-Behavioral Science Associates.

Rapoport, L. (1965). The state of crisis. In H. Parad (Ed.). *Crisis Intervention: Selected Readings.* NY: Family Service Association of America.

Richards, D. (2001). A field study of critical incident stress debriefing versus critical incident stress management. *Journal of Mental Health, 10,* 351-362.

Robinson, R. (2003). Personal communication.

Rose, S., Bisson, J., & Wessely, S. (2002). Psychological debriefing for preventing post traumatic stress disorder (PTSD). *The Cochrane Library,* Issue 1. Oxford, UK: Update Software.

Salmon, T.S. (1919). War neuroses and their lesson. *New York Medical Journal,* 108, 993-994.

Shapiro, D. A., & Shapiro, D. (1982). Meta-analysis of comparative therapy outcome studies. Psychological Bullentin, 92, 581-604.

Smith, M., Glass, G., & Miller, T. (1980). *The benefits of psychotherapy.* Baltimore: Johns Hopkins University Press.

Solomon, Z., & Benbenishty, R. (1986). The role of proximity, immediacy, and expectancy in frontline treatment of combat stress reaction among Israelis in the Lebanon War. *American Journal of Psychiatry,* 143, 613-617.

Strupp, H., Hadley, S., & Gomes-Schwartz, B. (1977). *Psychotherapy for Better or Worse.* NY: Aronson.

Susser, E.S., Herman, D., & Aaron, B. (2002, August). Combating the terror of terrorism. *Scientific American,* 287, 72-77.

Swanson, W.C., & Carbon, J.B. (1989). Crisis intervention: Theory and technique. In Task Force Report of the American Psychiatric Association. *Treatments of Psychiatric Disorders.* Washington, D.C.: APA Press.

van Emmerick, A., Kamphuis, J., Hulsbosch, A., & Emmelkamp, P. (2002). Single session debriefing after psychological trauma: A meta-analysis. *Lancet,* 360, 766-771.

Wessely, S., Rose, S., & Bisson, J. (1998). A systematic review of brief psychological interventions (debriefing) for the treatment of immediate trauma related symptoms and the prevention of post traumatic stress disorder (Cochrane Review). *Cochrane Library,* Issue 3, Oxford, UK: Update Software.

International Journal of Emergency Mental Health, Vol. 7, No. 1, pp. 9-22 © 2005 Chevron Publishing ISSN 1522-4821

A Prospective Cohort Study of the Effectiveness of Employer-Sponsored Crisis Interventions after a Major Disaster

Joseph A. Boscarino
The New York Academy of Medicine and Mount Sinai School of Medicine

Richard E. Adams
New York Academy of Medicine

Charles R. Figley
Florida State University

ABSTRACT: *Postdisaster crisis interventions have been viewed by many as the appropriate and immediate approach to enhance psychological well-being among persons affected by large-scale traumatic events. Yet, studies and systematic reviews have challenged the effectiveness of these efforts. This article provides the first rigorous scientific evidence to suggest that postdisaster crisis interventions in the workplace significantly reduced mental health disorders and symptoms up to 2 years after the initial interventions. Until now, studies have neither focused on the effectiveness and safety of brief mental health services following disasters, or traumatic events generally, nor examined the long-term impact of these interventions across a spectrum of outcomes using a rigorous research design. The focus of this study was to examine the impact of brief mental health crisis interventions received at the worksite following the World Trade Center disaster (WTCD) among a random sample of New York adults. The data for the present study come from a prospective cohort study of 1,681 adults interviewed by telephone at 1 year and 2 years after this event. Results indicate that worksite crisis interventions offered by employers following the WTCD had a beneficial impact across a spectrum of outcomes, including reduced risks for binge drinking, alcohol dependence, PTSD symptoms, major depression, somatization, anxiety, and global impairment, compared with individuals who did not receive these interventions. In addition, it appeared that 2-3 brief sessions achieved the maximum benefit for most outcomes examined. Implications for postdisaster crisis interventions efforts are discussed. [International Journal of Emergency Mental Health, 2005, 7(1), pp. 9-22].*

KEY WORDS: *crisis interventions, emergency services, Critical Incident Stress Management, CISM, community disasters, alcohol abuse, depression, PTSD, mental health services, effectiveness study, outcomes research.*

Joseph A. Boscarino, Ph.D., MPH, Division of Health & Science Policy, The New York Academy of Medicine and the Departments of General Internal Medicine & Pediatrics, Mount Sinai School of Medicine, New York; Richard E. Adams, Ph.D., Division of Health & Science Policy, The New York Academy of Medicine; Charles R. Figley, Ph.D., School of Social Work, Florida State University and Florida State University, Traumatology Institute. This research was supported by a grant from the National Institute of Mental Health (Grant # R01 MH66403). Correspondence regarding this article should be addressed to Joseph A. Boscarino, Ph.D., MPH, Division of Health and Science Policy, Room 552; The New York Academy of Medicine, 1216 Fifth Avenue, New York, NY 10029-5293; Tel: 212-419-3551; Fax: 212-822-7369; E-mail: jboscarino@nyam. org

For many persons exposed to psychological trauma, these events often occur suddenly and unexpectedly, particularly when due to such events as homicides, suicides, motor vehicle accidents, and natural and man-made disasters. Although the psychological sequelae following these events often appear brief, studies suggest that community-wide disasters characterized by large-scale loss of life, extensive property damage, economic disruptions, and those related to human intent result in increased rates of mental health problems and psychological distress (Brewin, Andrews, & Valentine, 2000; Bromet & Dew, 1995; Green,

1991; Noji, 1997; Norris, 1992; North et al., 1999; Rubonis & Bickman, 1991). All of these elements were present in the terrorist attacks on the World Trade Center in New York City (NYC) on September 11, 2001 (Boscarino, Galea, Ahren, Resnick, & Vlahov, 2002; Centers for Disease Control and Prevention [CDC], 2002; Galea et al., 2002). Research 6-months postdisaster suggested that while these symptoms resolved over time, many persons not directly affected by the attacks developed some symptoms (Boscarino, Galea, et al., 2004; Galea et al., 2003). Paradoxically, however, initial surveys after this event indicated that only small population-level increases occurred in mental health service utilization (Boscarino, Galea, Ahern, Resnick, & Vlahov, 2002; Boscarino, Galea, Ahern, Resnick, & Vlahov, 2003; Boscarino, Galea, et al., 2004).

Thus, despite the availability of mental health services in the NYC area following the attacks, major increases in mental health treatment-seeking failed to materialize (Boscarino, Adams, & Figley, 2004). While postdisaster mental health service utilization has been documented before the World Trade Center disaster (WTCD) (Boscarino et al., 2002), few studies have focused on population-level services utilization (Burkle, 1996; Gleser, Green, & Winget, 1981), which is required for disaster planning and preparedness. Within this context, to our knowledge few studies have focused on the effectiveness and safety of brief mental health services following disasters that might effectively mitigate the harmful effects of these events, or traumatic events generally. Moreover, as we note below, existing crisis intervention studies have failed to examine the long-term impact of these interventions across a spectrum of mental health outcomes and, in addition, rarely have done this using a rigorous observational research design.

The focus of this study was to examine the impact of brief mental health crisis interventions received by New Yorkers at the worksite following the WTCD event. Our investigation was part of a larger, federally-funded program of research focusing on the immediate and long-term effects of the WTCD among NYC residents. For the current study, specifically, we wanted to investigate whether participation in worksite crisis intervention services provided by area employers had a positive or negative long-term impact among the participants. As discussed below, we defined worksite crisis intervention as any brief sessions related to coping with the World Trade Center disaster shortly after this event directed by a mental health professional or counselor arranged by area employers for their employees.

These crisis interventions included what is generally termed "Critical Incident Stress Management" (CISM) (Boudreaux & McCabe, 2000), psychological debriefing (Kaplan, Iancu, & Bodner, 2001), and other focused, short-term interventions designed to provide emergency mental health services for trauma victims (Everly, Flannery, & Mitchell, 2000; Flannery & Everly, 2004; Mitchell, 2004). In the current study, approximately 7% of New Yorkers reported receiving brief crisis interventions at the worksite following the WTCD attacks.

Crisis interventions following traumatic events have been utilized for many years (Boudreaux & McCabe, 2000; Kaplan et al., 2001; Mitchell, 2004). However, the effectiveness and safety of these interventions following these events have been debated (Castellano, 2003; Flannery & Everly, 2000; Hokanson & Wirth, 2000; Jacobs, Horne-Moyer, & Jones, 2004; Kaplan et al., 2001; Luna, 2002; Mitchell, 2003). Nevertheless, group crisis interventions are commonly recommended following traumatic events (Flannery & Everly, 2004; Mitchell, 2004). Unfortunately, the true impact of these interventions has been hampered by both mixed study results (Bledsoe, 2003; Flannery & Everly, 2004) and, by conventional epidemiological standards, a lack of methodological research rigor for the studies actually conducted (Hulley et al., 2001).

METHODS

Study Participants

The data for the present study come from a prospective cohort study of English- or Spanish-speaking NYC adults who were living in NYC on the day of the WTCD. Using random-digit dialing, we conducted a baseline telephone survey a year after the attacks. Upon reaching a person at a residential telephone number, interviewers obtained verbal consent for the survey. If more than one eligible adult lived in the household, interviewers selected one based on the person with the most recent birthday. As part of the overall study, we over-sampled residents who reported receiving any mental health treatment in the year after the attacks. The population was also stratified by the 5 NYC boroughs and sampled proportionately. Questionnaires were translated into Spanish and then back-translated by bilingual Americans to ensure the linguistic and cultural appropriateness of the survey. Interviews for the baseline survey occurred between October and December 2002. For the follow-up survey, we attempted to re-interview all baseline participants one year later (i.e., 2 years after the WTCD). All follow-up interviews occurred between October 2003 and February 2004.

The data collection procedures were the same for both survey waves. Trained interviewers using a computer-assisted telephone interviewing system conducted the interviews. All interviewers were supervised and monitored by the survey contractor in collaboration with the investigative staff. A protocol was in place to provide mental health assistance to participants who required psychiatric counseling. The mean duration of the interviews was 45 minutes for the baseline and 35 minutes for follow-up interviews. The Institutional Review Board of The New York Academy of Medicine reviewed and approved the study's protocols.

For the baseline, 2,368 individuals completed the survey. We were able to re-interview 1,681 of these respondents in the follow-up survey. Approximately, 7% of the interviews were conducted in Spanish in the baseline and 5% in the follow-up survey. Using industry standards (American Association for Public Opinion Research, 2000), the baseline cooperation rate was approximately 63% (Boscarino, Adams, et al., 2004), and the re-interview rate for the follow-up study was 71%. A sampling weight was developed for each wave to correct for potential selection bias related to the number of telephone numbers and persons per household and for the over-sampling of treatment-seeking respondents. In addition, as we discuss below, demographic weights were used for the follow-up survey data to adjust for differences in response rates by different demographic groups.

An analysis comparing our weighted baseline sample to the Census data for NYC indicated no differences for age, gender, race, or NYC Borough (Adams & Boscarino, 2005). Thus, the baseline sample appeared to be representative of NYC and was not demographically biased due to the cooperation rate or sample selection. When we compared responders for the follow-up survey to non-responders (unweighted), however, we found Whites, older respondents, and women more likely to participate in this survey, which is not uncommon for longitudinal surveys (Kessler, Little, & Groves, 1995).

To correct for this potential bias, we adjusted our follow-up data for these differences using sampling weights derived from baseline data–the recommended method in this situation (Groves et al., 2004; Kessler et al., 1995). After weighting, a comparison between the baseline and the follow-up samples indicated no differences for age, gender, race, or NYC Borough, indicating that the weights corrected for differing participation rates for these four demographic groups. All analyses were conducted applying these weights, which allowed us to treat the longitudinal sample as a random, representative sample of NYC adult residents living in NYC on the day of the WTCD.

Health Outcomes Assessed

In our analyses, we included outcome measures related to both alcohol abuse and mental health status. Consistent with previous surveys and standardized measures used in epidemiologic studies of alcohol abuse (Allen & Columbus, 1995; Grieger, Fullerton, & Ursano, 2003), in the follow-up survey we asked respondents how many times during the past year they had 6 or more alcoholic drinks on a single occasion to measure binge-drinking behaviors. We then classified this response as less than "monthly/never" (coded 0) and "monthly or more" (coded 1). In the follow-up survey we also inquired about the respondent's consumption of alcoholic beverages based on the CAGE criteria for alcohol dependence (Magruder-Habib, Stevens, & Alling, 1993), a widely used and validated scale for alcoholism screening (King, 1986). Using these data, we defined respondents as meeting criteria for alcohol dependence if they had 2 or more positive responses on the CAGE scale (e.g., criticized about drinking, drank first thing in the morning, etc.). We then created a variable for meeting the CAGE criteria for the 12 months between the baseline and the follow-up interviews (coded 1) and not meeting the CAGE criteria during this period as the reference group (coded 0).

Our third study outcome related to symptoms for PTSD assessed during the follow-up survey. Since there were relatively few respondents who met full DSM-IV (American Psychiatric Association [APA], 1994) criteria for past year PTSD, we assessed a broader measure commonly referred to as sub-clinical or partial-PTSD. This measure has been described in detail elsewhere (Breslau, Lucia, & Davis, 2004). Essentially, respondents met criteria for sub-clinical PTSD if they experienced at least one symptom from each symptom group (B, C, and D) and the symptoms lasted at least one month in duration. We used this measure to identify individuals who suffered from PTSD symptoms but did not necessarily meet full criteria. Although these cases fail to meet the full criteria for PTSD, they nevertheless have significantly more impairment and problems with work and social relationships than those with few or no PTSD symptoms (Breslau et al., 2004). Thus, we utilized this partial PTSD measure as an indicator of psychological problems related to trauma exposure.

Our PTSD measure was developed for telephone administration and used in previous national surveys (Kilpatrick et al., 2003; Resnick, Kilpatrick, Dansky, Saunders, & Best, 1993) as well as in recent WTCD studies (Boscarino et al., 2002; Boscarino et al., 2003; Boscarino, Adams, et al., 2004; Boscarino, Figley, et al., 2004; Boscarino, Galea, et al., 2004). Cronbach's alpha for the symptoms used in this scale was 0.90 (Boscarino et al., 2002). In addition, data related to the validity of our PTSD scale have been previously reported and suggest that this scale can successfully diagnosis PTSD (Boscarino, Adams, et al., 2004; Kilpatrick, et al., 1998). To date, versions of this PTSD scale have been used in mental health surveys involving over 15,000 telephone interviews (Acierno et al., 2000; Boscarino, Adams, et al., 2004; Boscarino, Figley, et al., 2004; Boscarino, Galea, et al., 2004; Galea et al., 2003; Kilpatrick et al., 2003; Resnick et al., 1993).

Our fourth outcome measure in the follow-up survey assessed the occurrence of major depression in the past year. To classify respondents for this diagnosis, we used a version of the SCID's major depressive disorder scale from the non-patients version (Spitzer, Williams, & Gibbon, 1987), which has also been used in telephone-based population surveys (Acierno et al., 2000; Boscarino, Adams, et al., 2004; Boscarino, Figley, et al., 2004; Boscarino, Galea, et al., 2004; Galea et al., 2002; Kilpatrick et al., 2003). Following DSM-IV criteria (APA, 1994), respondents met the criteria for depression if they had five or more depression symptoms for at least two-weeks in the past 12 months. In the current study, Cronbach's alpha for the 10 symptoms used in this scale was 0.87. Data related to the validity of this scale were also previously reported and suggested that this scale can successfully diagnose depression in the general population (Boscarino, Adams, et al., 2004; Boscarino, Figley, et al., 2004; Boscarino, Galea, et al., 2004).

In our follow-up, we also assessed the occurrence of 3 psychiatric syndromes in the past 30 days based on the Brief Symptom Inventory-18 (BSI-18), a self-reported psychiatric scale derived from the Hopkins Symptom Checklist (Derogatis, 2001). The measure contained 18 items divided into 4 subscales relating to somatization, anxiety, depression, and global severity. For the current study, we present results for the somatization, anxiety, and the global severity scales. The BSI-18 has been standardized based on a national community sample and has clinical T-scores to define cases. We used a T-score of 65 or higher for case definition, representing a symptom score above the 90th percentile. Cronbach's alphas for BSI-18 scales range from 0.74 to 0.89 and test-retest correlations range from 0.68 to 0.90 (Derogatis, 2001). The BSI-18 has been validated against the widely used SCL-90R psychiatric scale and has been shown to have diagnostic properties consistent with this instrument (Derogatis, 2001).

Crisis Interventions Assessed

Since assessing the effects of brief crisis interventions at the work site was a key component of our study design, the survey queried respondents about participation in this type of service during the baseline survey. Specifically, we asked, "Since the World Trade Center disaster, have you attended any brief sessions related to coping with the World Trade Center disaster conducted by a mental health professional or counselor that were arranged by your employer or an organization such as a community group or religious group?" The overwhelming majority who attended these sessions (70%) indicated that they were at the worksite. We classified respondents who attended these worksite sessions as the brief crisis intervention group ($n = 180$) and all others as the non-intervention group ($n = 1,501$). (Those attending brief crisis interventions at other locations only were not classified as worksite crisis intervention cases.)

We also inquired about the number of times the respondent attended these brief sessions and the content of the sessions attended (e.g., educated you about severe stress symptoms, taught you to relax, discussed the event, had you think about the event, etc.). Based on the number of reported sessions attended, respondents were classified into the following categories: no worksite session attended ($n = 1,501$); one session attended ($n = 82$); 2-3 sessions attended ($n = 68$); and 4 or more worksite sessions attended ($n = 30$), with no worksite sessions attended designated as the reference category. Finally, we asked the treatment group to what extent these brief sessions help them deal with emotional problems they may have had since the WTCD. The response categories were "not at all," "a little," "some," and "a lot."

Study Control Variables

Since this was a population-based, observational study design without random assignment to treatment or control groups, we statistically controlled for potential selection bias and confounding variables that could have affected our results (Cohen & Cohen, 1983; Hulley et al., 2001). These included demographic factors, history of stressor exposures, mental health history, and psychological resource factors. It should be noted, however, that since these worksite treatments were not sought out directly by employees, but provided by area employers as an "employee assistance" program, self-selection bias should not be as problematic, compared with developing a covariate model for those who actually sought postdisaster mental health treatment in the community (Boscarino, Adams, et al., 2004). In the latter situation, the study results would likely be heavily biased by patient self-selection to treatment (Hulley et al, 2001.)

Demographic Characteristics. We included five demographic factors as study control variables in our study, including age, education, gender, marital status, and race/ethnicity. Age was coded into four categories, 18-29, 30-44, 45-64, and 65+, with 65+ as the reference category. Education, gender, and marital status were coded as follows: non-college graduate vs. college graduate, male vs. female, and not married vs. married (including living together), with non-college graduate, male, and not married coded as the reference category. Consistent with most population research (Breslau et al., 1998; Ortega, Rosenheck, Alegria, & Desai, 2000), race/ethnicity was self-identified in the following manner. First, the survey interviewer asked the respondent if he/she was of Spanish or Hispanic origin. Next, interviewers queried the respondent about his/her race, which included White, Black or African American, Asian, Native Hawaiian or other Pacific Islander, American Indian or Alaska Native, or "some other race." Using the responses to these two questions, we classified all respondents as follows: non-Hispanic White, non-Hispanic Black or African American, Hispanic, and Other Race/No Race Given. Non-Hispanic White was the reference category. All of the demographic variables were from the baseline study, unless the data were missing, in which case the follow-up data were substituted.

Stress Exposure, Risk Factors, and Psychological Resources. Our analyses included three stressor variables that may have placed the individual at higher risk for poor mental health and two psychological resources that may have lowered such risk. The baseline survey inquired about 14 pos-

sible events (yes; no) that the respondent could have experienced during the WTC attacks. Since there was not an a priori method of assessing the severity of any of these event exposures, we summed these events into a WTCD exposure scale. We then coded these events into low exposure (0-1 event), moderate exposure (2-3 events), high exposure (4-5 events), and very high exposure (6+ events). Low exposure was the reference category. Second, a traumatic events measure focused on 10 lifetime traumatic events (Freedy, Kilpatrick, & Resnick, 1993), other than the WTCD, which could have happened to the respondent before the WTCD (e.g., forced sexual contact, being attacked with a weapon, having a serious accident, etc.). Respondents were coded into one of four categories, including no lifetime traumas, 1 trauma, 2-3 traumas, and 4 or more traumas, with no traumas coded as the reference category.

The social psychological resource variables were social support (Sherbourne & Stewart, 1991) and self-esteem (Rosenberg, 1979), both of which were collected during the baseline survey. Social support (Cronbach's alpha = .83) was the sum of four questions about emotional, informational, and instrumental support (e.g., someone available to help you if you were confined to bed). Based on an examination of the scale's frequency distribution, we coded respondents into approximately three equal size groups: low, moderate, and high social support. The second resource measure, self-esteem, was measured by the Rosenberg's self-esteem scale (Rosenberg, 1979). The scale (Cronbach's alpha = .73) was the sum of five items in the original scale (e.g., I certainly feel useless at times. On the whole, I am satisfied with myself.). The response options were "strongly agree" (coded 1) to "strongly disagree" (coded 4). We coded items so that high scores reflected high self-esteem. The scale had a highly skewed frequency distribution, with over 70% of the respondents having scores between 17 and 20. Therefore, we divided respondents into three categories: low (5-17), moderate (18-19), and high self-esteem (20). For these resource variables, low social support and low self-esteem were the reference categories. These stress/risk and resource measures were used and validated in other WTCD studies in New York City (Boscarino, Adams, et al., 2004; Boscarino, Galea, et al., 2004; Galea et al., 2002).

History of Lifetime Depression. We also included a measure of the lifetime occurrence of one or more episodes of major depression as a control variable to adjust for a history of mental illness. To classify respondents for this diagnosis, as noted above, we used a version of the SCID's major depressive disorder scale from the non-patients version (Spitzer, Williams, & Gibbon, 1987), which has also been used in telephone-based population surveys (Acierno et al., 2000; Boscarino, Adams, et al., 2004; Boscarino, Figley, et al, 2004; Boscarino, Galea, et al., 2004; Galea et al., 2002; Kilpatrick et al., 2003). Following DSM-IV criteria (APA, 1994), respondents met the criteria for lifetime major depression if they had five or more depression symptoms for at least two-weeks in their lifetimes. As previously noted, the reliability and validity of this scale suggested that it could be used to diagnose depression in the general population (Boscarino, Adams, et al., 2004; Boscarino, Galea, et al., 2004).

Statistical Analyses

Our analytic strategy proceeded in several steps. First, we present descriptive statistics for the sample and for our 7 outcome variables of interest. We next compare the descriptive characteristics for the crisis intervention group ($N = 180$) to the non-intervention group ($N = 1,501$) and then test for statistically significant differences between them. We then describe the characteristics of the crisis intervention services received. Finally, we estimate a series of logistic regression models whereby we regressed each of the 7 outcomes measures of interest separately on the crisis intervention status, demographic, stress/risk, and resource variables discussed. These regression models, thus, assess the impact of brief worksite crisis counseling for the 7 mental health outcomes examined, controlling for selection biases and confounding variables that could obscure these associations (Cohen & Cohen, 1983; Hulley et al., 2001; Neter, Wasserman, & Kutner, 1990). If the baseline crisis intervention sessions were successful, then we would expect to see odds ratios (ORs) less than 1, suggesting that the crisis interventions were protective for the adverse outcomes examined. In addition, given the research literature discussed (Boudreaux & McCabe, 2000; Kaplan et al., 2001), we expected to see a beneficial treatment effect after 1-3 crisis sessions.

For all analyses, we use the survey estimation (svy) command in Stata, version 7 (Stata Corporation, 2001), to generate frequency distributions, point estimates, and our final multivariate regression models. This command set is required for complex surveys and uses the first-order Taylor series linear approximation method (Stata Corporation, 2001). This estimation procedure adjusts the data to take into account our sampling design, which included case weights to adjust

for potentially over-representing persons in households with more telephone lines per adult, the treatment over-sample, and the follow-up survey adjustment. Because of this survey estimation method, the N-values (unweighted) and percentages (weighted) may not be consistent in the tables presented. All p-values presented are based on 2-tail tests.

RESULTS

Descriptive statistics for the study sample are presented in Table 1. First, as can be seen, residents of NYC tend to be fairly educated, with over 40% having a college degree. About 50% were married or living together, and the majority were classified as nonwhite. In terms of our stress/risk measures, overall almost 75% of the respondents reported experiencing 2 or more WTCD related events, almost 70% reported at least one lifetime trauma experience, other than the WTCD, and 19% met criteria for lifetime major depression. These results were comparable to those found in other surveys of the WTCD in NYC (Galea et al., 2002; Vlahov, Galea, Ahern, Resnick, Boscarino, et al., 2004; Vlahov, Galea, Ahern, Resnick, & Kilpatrick, 2004).

In addition, most participants were classified as having moderate to high social support and scored in the moderate to high range on the self-esteem scale, based on the cut points selected for these scales (Boscarino, Adams, et al., 2004). In terms of any difference between the intervention vs. the non-intervention group, only 2 variables examined were statistically significant at the $p < 0.05$ level. These included level of education and WTCD exposure status ($p < 0.001$ for both), whereby the intervention group had higher education and WTCD exposure levels. This makes sense and suggests the companies nearer the disaster site (e.g., Wall Street) were more likely to provide these services for employees.

Overall, 7% (95% confidence interval [C.I.] = 5.6-8.3) of our sample, representing approximately 420,000 New York City adults, reported that they had received some type of brief crisis intervention services at the worksite conducted by a mental health professional following the WTCD (Table 2). Of those who received these sessions, most individuals, about 85%, attended between 1 and 3 sessions. As is common with these interventions (Boudreaux & McCabe, 2000; Kaplan et al., 2001), the content of these sessions covered a range of topics. Between 60% and 70% of the respondents reported that they were instructed about stress symptoms, coping and relaxation techniques, and strategies for how to think positively. The sessions also covered how to stop

Table 1.
Study Population Descriptive Statistics (N =1,681)

Independent Variables	All Respondents Weighted % (Unweighted N) (N = 1,681)	95% CI	Intervention Weighted % (Unweighted N) (N = 180)	No Intervention Weighted % (Unweighted N) (N = 1,501)	$\chi2$ (p-value)
Age					
18-29	22.7 (284)	20.1-25.6	24.1 (35)	22.6 (249)	9.48 (0.106)
30-44	32.9 (596)	30.1-35.8	43.2 (83)	32.1 (513)	
45-64	32.5 (586)	29.8-35.4	27.3 (58)	32.9 (528)	
65+	11.9 (215)	10.1-13.9	5.4 (4)	12.4 (211)	
Education					
Non-College Graduate	58.3 (906)	55.4-61.2	36.7 (55)	59.9 (851)	23.88 (<0.001)
College Graduate	41.7 (775)	38.8-44.6	63.3 (125)	40.1 (650)	
Gender					
Male	46.2 (693)	43.2-49.3	37.7 (63)	46.8 (630)	3.60 (0.089)
Female	53.8 (988)	50.7-56.9	62.3 (117)	53.2 (871)	
Marital Status					
Not Married	49.7 (972)	46.7-52.7	48.6 (98)	49.8 (874)	0.06 (0.831)
Married	50.3 (709)	47.3-53.3	51.4 (82)	50.2 (627)	
Race					
White	43.0 (782)	40.1-45.9	45.7 (87)	42.7 (695)	2.28 (0.567)
African American	26.0 (422)	23.4-28.7	20.1 (41)	26.4 (381)	
Latino	24.1 (367)	21.5-26.9	27.0 (37)	23.9 (330)	
Other	7.0 (110)	5.6-8.7	7.2 (15)	7.0 (95)	
Exposure to WTCD					
Low (0-1 events)	26.7 (362)	24.0-29.6	5.8 (9)	28.3 (353)	73.21 (<0.001)
Moderate (2-3 events)	43.9 (719)	40.9-47.0	34.6 (61)	44.6 (658)	
High (4-5 events)	21.8 (416)	19.4-24.4	36.9 (62)	20.7 (354)	
Very High (6+ events)	7.6 (184)	6.3-9.1	22.7 (48)	6.5 (136)	
Lifetime Traumatic Events					
0 events	33.6 (466)	30.7-36.6	24.8 (38)	34.2 (428)	8.59 (0.073)
1 event	23.4 (400)	20.9-26.1	21.9 (41)	23.5 (359)	
2-3 events	26.7 (484)	24.2-29.5	28.6 (52)	26.7 (432)	
4+ events	16.2 (331)	14.2-18.4	24.7 (49)	15.6 (282)	
Lifetime Depression					
No	81.2 (1243)	79.0-83.3	74.3 (123)	81.8 (1120)	3.91 (0.055)
Yes	18.8 (438)	16.7-21.1	25.7 (57)	18.3 (381)	
Social Support					
Low	34.3 (573)	31.4-37.3	24.2 (43)	35.1 (530)	6.05 (0.085)
Moderate	36.9 (636)	34.0-39.9	40.3 (77)	36.7 (559)	
High	28.8 (472)	26.1-31.6	35.6 (60)	28.3 (412)	
Self-Esteem					
Low	32.2 (613)	29.4-35.0	27.3 (49)	32.5 (564)	1.39 (0.562)
Moderate	25.0 (408)	22.4-27.8	27.6 (51)	24.8 (357)	
High	42.9 (660)	39.9-45.9	45.2 (80)	42.7 (580)	

Note: CI = confidence interval

Table 2.
Baseline Crisis Interventions Descriptive Statistics (N = 1,681)

Intervention Characteristics	% (Weighted)	95% CI	N (Unweighted)
Number of Brief Crisis Sessions			
None	93.1	91.7-94.4	1501
One	3.8	2.9-5.2	82
Two to Three	2.2	1.7-3.0	68
Four or more	0.8	0.5-1.2	30
Content of Brief Sessions (for those having sessions)			
Educated about Stress Symptoms	71.2	61.1-79.6	137
Talked about Experiences	67.0	56.3-76.2	134
Taught to Cope with Things	69.4	59.8-77.6	127
Taught to Think Positively	64.4	54.7-73.1	116
Taught to Stop Bad Thoughts	45.7	36.1-55.6	81
Taught to Evaluate Thoughts	56.6	46.7-66.1	99
Taught to Deal with Emotions	69.1	59.4-77.3	127
Taught to Relax	68.2	58.6-76.5	127
Reported Helpfulness of Crisis Intervention (for those having sessions)			
Not at All Helpful	22.4	14.1-33.6	31
Helped a Little	33.7	24.5-44.2	57
Helped Some	22.8	16.3-31.0	44
Helped a Lot	21.2	15.0-29.0	48

Note: CI = confidence interval

negative thoughts, how to evaluate thoughts, and how to deal with one's emotions. Lastly, over 80% of the respondents reported that these brief counseling sessions had helped them to deal, at least to some degree, with emotional problems related to the WTCD (Table 2).

The percentages of respondents meeting the diagnostic criteria for the 7 outcomes assessed are shown in Table 3. Almost 15% of the sample met the criteria for binge drinking in the previous 12 months, while about 3% met criteria for alcohol dependence on the GAGE scale during this time period. In terms of the psychological status, 8% met criteria for sub-clinical PTSD, and about 12% met criteria for a major depressive episode in the past 12 months. In addition, 11%, 9%, and 9% met the criteria for BSI-18 somatization, anxiety,

and global severity symptoms in the past 30 days, respectively (Table 3).

The logistic regression results presented next show the impact of the baseline crisis interventions on our study outcomes during the follow-up period, 1-year after the baseline study (i.e., 2-years after the attacks), adjusted for potential selection bias and confounding factors (Table 4). As can be seen, in terms of binge drinking (OR = 0.26, $p < 0.05$) and alcohol dependence (OR = 0.09, $p < 0.05$) between 1 and 3 sessions appeared to be effective in protecting workers from these adverse outcomes during the follow-up. Consistent with previous findings (Pfefferbaum & Doughty, 2001; Vlahov, Galea, Ahern, Resnick, Boscarino, et al., 2004), alcohol abusers in our study generally tended to be male and younger.

In terms of PTSD and depression during the follow-up period, it appears that 2-3 sessions were protective for these outcomes, with an OR = 0.36 ($p < 0.05$) and an OR = 0.23 ($p < 0.05$) for PTSD and major depression, respectively. Consistent with previous studies (Boscarino, Adams, et al., 2004; Galea et al., 2002), middle-aged respondents, Latinos, individuals exposed to more WTCD events, those who experienced more lifetime traumas, participants who met criteria for lifetime depression, and individuals with low self-esteem were more likely to experience symptoms consistent with sub-clinical PTSD, compared with older, White, low WTCD exposure, no history of trauma, no history of depression, or higher self-esteem adults. Again consistent with previous findings (Boscarino, Adams, et al., 2004; Galea et al., 2002), depression was associated with being older, Latino, higher exposure to WTCD events, and low self-esteem. As one would expect, lifetime depression was related to depression past year. Interestingly, once other factors were controlled, gender did not predict this outcome.

In terms of the 30-day BSI-18 outcomes for somatization, anxiety, and global severity during the study follow-up period, once again it seemed that 2-3 brief interventions sessions were successful in protecting New York adults from these adverse outcomes, with ORs equal to 0.36 ($p < 0.05$), 0.17 ($p < 0.01$), and 0.30 ($p < 0.05$), respectively. As can be seen, somatization tended to be positively associated with women, African Americans/Latinos, higher WTCD exposures, and lifetime depression, but negatively associated with younger adults and higher levels of social support (Table 4). BSI-18 anxiety tended to be positively associated with adults 45-64, Latinos, higher WTCD exposures, and lifetime depression, but negatively associated with higher education, higher social support, and higher self-esteem (Table 4). Finally, BSI-18 global severity tended to be positively associated with Latinos, higher WTCD exposures, and lifetime depression, but again, negatively associated with younger age, higher education, higher social support, and higher self-esteem (Table 4).

Table 3.
Descriptive Statistics for Follow-up Mental Health Outcomes Assessed ($N = 1,681$)

Follow-up Dependent Variables	% (Weighted)	95% CI	N (Unweighted)
Any Binge Drinking Past Year			
No	85.1	82.7-87.1	1448
Yes	14.9	12.9-17.3	233
Alcohol Dependence Past Year			
No	97.3	96.3-98.1	1625
Yes	2.7	1.9-3.7	56
Sub-clinical (partial) PTSD Past Year			
No	91.9	90.2-93.3	1496
Yes	8.1	6.7-9.8	185
Major Depression Past Year			
No	88.4	86.6-90.1	1404
Yes	11.6	9.9-13.4	277
BSI-18: Somatization Past 30 Days			
No	88.8	86.9-90.4	1432
Yes	11.2	9.6-13.2	249
BSI-18: Anxiety Past 30 Days			
No	90.9	89.2-92.4	1464
Yes	9.1	7.6-10.9	217
BSI-18: Global Severity Past 30 Days			
No	91.3	89.6-92.7	1470
Yes	8.7	7.3-10.4	211

Note: CI = confidence interval

DISCUSSION

Based on our analyses, it appears that worksite crisis interventions provided by many NYC employers following the events of September 11, 2001, had a beneficial impact on the mental status of employees across a spectrum of outcomes. As was seen, these outcomes included a significant reduced risk for binge drinking, alcohol dependence, PTSD symptoms, major depression, somatization, anxiety, and global impairment, compared with comparable individuals who did not receive these interventions. In addition, it appeared that 2-3 brief sessions achieved the maximum benefit for most of the outcomes we examined. The consistency of our results across all the outcomes examined surprised us but we think reinforces the significance of our findings. In addition, we also assessed our results by including the baseline measure for each respective outcome assessed, a very conservative approach, given that our outcomes variables were dichotomous (Hulley et al., 2001). These findings were consistent with the results shown in Table 4.

Thus, the WTCD event in New York City seems to have provided an opportunity to evaluate a natural experiment in mental health services delivery. A significant number of NYC employers brought in crisis intervention teams to provide mental health services to employees at the worksite. Our previous research had shown that the majority of adults in NYC did not seek mental health services in the community following the WTCD event, even though they may have benefited and these were provided for free by different agencies (Boscarino et al., 2002; Boscarino, Adams, et al., 2004). Our current study suggests, however, that those who did receive brief worksite crisis intervention counseling provided by employers clearly benefited as many as 2 years after the WTCD event.

A study limitation, of course, was that our study was not based on random assignment of cases to an intervention vs. a control group (Hulley et al., 2001). Instead, some employers elected to provide crisis interventions for their employees. In addition, the provision of these services was not completely random, as we noted above for education and WTCD exposure levels. We attempted to control for these potential biases, statistically, by inclusion of key demographic, stressor exposure, mental health history, and for social and psychological resource variables as covariates in our logistic regression models. Nevertheless, it is possible that our results may still be biased (Hulley et al.).

Other possible limitations include the fact that we omitted individuals without a telephone and those who did not speak either English or Spanish. Given that the sample matched the 2000 Census for NYC (Adams & Boscarino, 2005), the absence of these households did not appear to have introduced any overall demographic bias. Nevertheless, we are limited in generalizing to other ethnic/language groups in NYC. Another limitation, of course, was that while our mental health measures were based on standardized and validated scales and our treatment exposure variable was based on pre-tested and standardized survey questions, these variables, nevertheless, were based on self-report and therefore may be biased because of recall errors or for other reasons.

Despite these limitations, however, it appears that brief crisis interventions at the worksite following the WTCD event were clinically effective up to 2 years after treatment. As we noted, the focus of this study was to examine the effectiveness and safety of brief mental health crisis interventions received by New Yorkers at the worksite following the WTCD event. In the current study, approximately 7% of New Yorkers reported receiving brief crisis interventions at the worksite following the WTCD event. As indicated, postdisaster crisis interventions have been in use for some time. However, the effectiveness and safety of these crisis interventions have been debated. While we plan to continue our evaluation of these interventions, our current research suggests that these emergency services were highly effective for New Yorkers up to 2 years after the World Trade Center disaster. Based on our current findings, we suggest that crisis intervention services should be considered as a first line of emergency management for those potentially affected by large-scale community disasters.

Table 4.
Multivariate Logistic Regressions for Crisis Intervention Exposures at Baseline Predicting Outcomes at 2-Year follow-up, Controlling for Demographic, Stress/Risk, and Resource Variables.

	Binge Drinking OR (95% CI)	Alcohol Dependence OR (95% CI)	Sub-Clinical (partial) PTSD OR (95% CI)	Major Depression OR (95% CI)	BSI-18 Somatization OR (95% CI)	BSI-18 Anxiety OR (95% CI)	BSI-18 Global Severity OR (95% CL)
Brief Crisis Sessions							
None (Ref)	1.00 —	1.00 —	1.00 —	1.00 —	1.00 —	1.00 —	1.00 —
1 Time	0.42 (0.17-1.03)	0.09 (0.01-0.82)*	0.89 (0.28-2.87)	1.21 (0.36-4.02)	0.45 (0.15-1.28)	0.52 (0.08-3.23)	0.66 (0.10-4.38)
2-3 Times	0.26 (0.08-0.85)*	0.19 (0.02-1.56)	0.36 (0.13-0.98)*	0.23 (0.07-0.71)*	0.36 (0.15-0.88)*	0.17 (0.05-0.61)**	0.30 (0.09-0.99)*
4 or more times	0.61 (0.18-2.05)	0.67 (0.11-4.18)	1.32 (0.46-3.73)	1.32 (0.40-4.42)	1.05 (0.31-3.62)	1.36 (0.38-4.90)	1.51 (0.40-5.67)
Demographic Variables							
Age							
18-29	3.27 (1.57-6.81)**	0.97 (0.24-3.86)	1.06 (0.35-3.21)	1.26 (0.53-3.01)	0.10 (0.04-0.28)***	0.60 (0.20-1.82)	0.24 (0.09-0.66)**
30-44	2.49 (1.24-5.00)*	1.10 (0.31-3.90)	3.52 (1.53-8.09)**	3.34 (1.61-6.93)***	0.52 (0.29-1.03)	2.32 (0.94-5.71)	0.76 (0.35-1.64)
45-64	1.82 (0.91-3.62)	1.19 (0.36-3.92)	2.79 (1.26-6.17)*	2.73 (1.35-5.58)**	1.02 (0.55-1.88)	2.51 (1.04-6.03)*	1.39 (0.68-2.84)
65+ (Ref)	1.00 —	1.00 —	1.00 —	1.00 —	1.00 —	1.00 —	1.00 —
Education							
Non-Grad (Ref)	1.00 —	1.00 —	1.00 —	1.00 —	1.00 —	1.00 —	1.00 —
College Graduate	0.84 (0.56-1.25)	1.93 (0.95-3.92)	1.22 (0.74-2.00)	0.85 (0.56-1.29)	0.65 (0.39-1.06)	0.52 (0.33-0.83)**	0.39 (0.23-0.66)***
Gender							
Male (Ref)	1.00 —	1.00 —	1.00 —	1.00 —	1.00 —	1.00 —	1.00 —
Female	0.29 (0.20-0.43)***	0.32 (0.16-0.63)***	1.38 (0.86-2.22)	0.90 (0.60-1.33)	1.63 (1.03-2.56)*	0.93 (0.58-1.49)	0.61 (0.38-1.00)
Marital Status							
Not Married (Ref)	1.00 —	1.00 —	1.00 —	1.00 —	1.00 —	1.00 —	1.00 —
Married	0.93 (0.64-1.35)	0.59 (0.28-1.23)	0.80 (0.50-1.27)	0.93 (0.62-1.39)	0.66 (0.43-1.03)	0.74 (0.45-1.24)	0.70 (0.43-1.16)
Race							
White (Ref)	1.00 —	1.00 —	1.00 —	1.00 —	1.00 —	1.00 —	1.00 —
African American	0.78 (0.47-1.29)	2.54 (1.00-6.45)	1.46 (0.79-2.71)	1.37 (0.82-2.30)	1.77 (1.04-3.08)*	1.16 (0.63-2.11)	1.34 (0.71-2.52)
Latino	1.86 (1.16-2.96)*	5.10 (1.78-14.58)**	2.97 (1.58-5.57)***	2.42 (1.42-4.14)***	3.24 (1.90-5.54)***	3.36 (1.93-5.86)***	4.28 (2.40-7.62)***
Other	0.94 (0.43-2.06)	2.22 (0.43-11.68)	0.74 (0.34-1.60)	0.60 (0.27-1.32)	1.30 (0.55-3.05)	1.62 (0.67-3.91)	2.67 (1.11-6.40)*
Stress/Risk Variables							
Exposure to WTCD							
Low (Ref)	1.00 —	1.00 —	1.00 —	1.00 —	1.00 —	1.00 —	1.00 —
Moderate	1.48 (0.90-2.41)	1.09 (0.41-2.89)	1.30 (0.67-2.47)	1.67 (0.96-2.90)	0.85 (0.49-1.46)	0.99 (0.53-1.85)	1.26 (0.69-2.28)
High	1.80 (1.03-3.13)*	1.84 (0.63-5.30)	1.73 (0.85-3.55)	2.08 (1.12-3.88)*	1.02 (0.54-1.94)	1.49 (0.75-2.94)	2.15 (1.07-4.30)*
Very High	1.53 (0.80-2.92)	2.16 (0.66-7.06)	2.86 (1.30-6.29)**	4.28 (2.10-8.70)***	2.34 (1.19-4.61)*	2.57 (1.17-5.64)*	4.17 (1.95-8.92)***
Lifetime Trauma							
0 events (Ref)	1.00 —	1.00 —	1.00 —	1.00 —	1.00 —	1.00 —	1.00 —
1 event	0.97 (0.58-1.62)	1.44 (0.51-4.10)	1.57 (0.74-3.30)	1.05 (0.55-1.98)	0.99 (0.53-1.85)	1.22 (0.64-2.34)	1.01 (0.52-1.94)
2-3 events	1.24 (0.76-2.03)	2.28 (0.76-6.85)	2.87 (1.50-5.51)**	1.60 (0.95-2.69)	1.67 (0.94-2.96)	1.68 (0.90-3.14)	0.97 (0.52-1.81)
4+ events	1.34 (0.79-2.28)	2.82 (0.96-8.26)	3.28 (1.64-6.58)***	1.64 (0.93-2.90)	1.28 (0.69-2.37)	1.42 (0.70-2.90)	0.97 (0.47-2.00)
Lifetime Depression							
No (Ref)	1.00 —	1.00 —	1.00 —	1.00 —	1.00 —	1.00 —	1.00 —
Yes	1.06 (0.69-1.63)	1.61 (0.73-3.54)	2.63 (1.64-4.25)***	3.72 (2.45-5.67)***	2.36 (1.50-3.70)***	3.12 (1.92-5.09)***	3.77 (2.28-6.23)***
Resource Variables							
Social Support							
Low (Ref)	1.00 —	1.00 —	1.00 —	1.00 —	1.00 —	1.00 —	1.00 —
Moderate	0.98 (0.64-1.52)	1.47 (0.63-3.46)	0.83 (0.51-1.35)	0.77 (0.50-1.20)	0.58 (0.37-0.89)*	0.49 (0.30-0.81)**	0.39 (0.24-0.62)***
High	0.76 (0.48-1.23)	3.26 (1.29-8.25)*	0.50 (0.25-0.97)*	0.71 (0.43-1.19)	0.53 (0.30-0.95)*	0.42 (0.23-0.78)**	0.54 (0.29-1.00)
Self-Esteem							
Low (Ref)	1.00 —	1.00 —	1.00 —	1.00 —	1.00 —	1.00 —	1.00 —
Moderate	0.58 (0.35-0.94)*	0.60 (0.24-1.52)	0.69 (0.39-1.22)	0.34 (0.21-0.56)***	0.83 (0.50-1.38)	0.43 (0.24-0.76)**	0.45 (0.26-0.77)**
High	0.74 (0.47-1.15)	0.61 (0.25-1.45)	0.42 (0.23-0.74)**	0.26 (0.16-0.43)***	0.36 (0.22-0.60)	0.20 (0.11-0.38)***	0.17 (0.09-0.33)***

NOTE: *p <.05   **p <.01   ***p <.001.   OR = odds ration,   CI = confidence interval,   Ref = reference group.

REFERENCES

Acierno R., Kilpatrick, D. G., Resnick, H., Saunders, B. E., De Arellano, M., & Best, C. (2000). Assault, PTSD, family substance use, and depression as risk factors for cigarette use in youth: Findings from the National Survey of Adolescents. *Journal of Traumatic Stress, 13,* 381-396.

Adams, R. E. & Boscarino, J. A. (2005). Stress and well-being in the aftermath of the World Trade Center attack: The continuing effects of a community-wide disaster. *Journal of Community Psychology, 33,* 175-190.

Allen, J. P. & Columbus, M. (1995). *Assessing alcohol problems: A guide for clinicians and researchers.* Bethesda, MD: National Institute on Alcohol Abuse and Alcoholism.

American Association for Public Opinion Research. (2000). *Standard definitions: Final dispositions of case codes and outcomes rates for surveys.* Ann Arbor, MI: Author.

American Psychiatric Association. (1994). *Diagnostic and statistical manual of mental disorders* (4th ed.). Washington, DC: Author.

Bledsoe, B. E. (2003). Critical incident stress management (CISM): Benefit or risk for emergency services? *Prehospital Emergency Care, 7,* 272-279.

Boscarino, J. A., Adams, R. E., & Figley, C. R. (2004). Mental health service use 1-year after the World Trade Center disaster: Implications for mental health care. *General Hospital Psychiatry, 26,* 346-358.

Boscarino, J. A., Figley, C. R., Adams, R. E., Galea, S., Resnick, H., Fleischman, A. R., et al. (2004). Adverse reactions associated with studying persons recently exposed to a mass urban disaster. *The Journal of Nervous and Mental Disease, 192,* 515-524.

Boscarino, J. A., Galea, S., Adams, R. E., Ahern, J., Resnick, H., & Vlahov, D. (2004). Mental health service and psychiatric medication use following the terrorist attacks in New York City. *Psychiatric Services, 55,* 274-283.

Boscarino, J. A., Galea, S., Ahern, J., Resnick, H., & Vlahov, D. (2002). Utilization of mental health services following the September 11th terrorist attacks in Manhattan, New York City. *International Journal of Emergency Mental Health, 4,* 143-155.

Boscarino, J. A., Galea, S., Ahern, J., Resnick, H., & Vlahov, D. (2003). Psychiatric medication use among Manhattan residents following the World Trade Center disaster. *Journal of Traumatic Stress, 16,* 301-306.

Boudreaux, E. D., & McCabe, B. (2000). Critical incident stress management: I. Interventions and effectiveness. *Psychiatric Services, 51,* 1095-1097.

Breslau, N., Kessler, R. C., Chilcoat, H. D., Schultz, L. R., Davis, G. C., & Andreski, P. (1998). Trauma and posttraumatic stress disorder in the community. *Archives of General Psychiatry, 55,* 626-632.

Breslau, N., Lucia, V. C., & Davis, G. C. (2004). Partial PTSD versus full PTSD: An empirical examination of associated impairment. *Psychological Medicine, 34,* 1205-1214.

Brewin, C. R., Andrews, B., & Valentine, J. D. (2000). Meta-analysis of risk factors for posttraumatic stress disorder in trauma-exposed adults. *Journal of Consulting and Clinical Psychology, 68,* 748-766.

Bromet, E. J. & Dew, M. A. (1995). Review of psychiatric epidemiologic research on disasters. *Epidemiologic Reviews, 17,* 113-119.

Burkle, F. M. (1996). Acute-phase mental health consequences of disasters: Implications for triage and emergency medical services. *Annals of Emergency Medicine, 28,* 119-128

Castellano, C. (2003). Large group crisis intervention for law enforcement in response to the September 11 World Trade Center mass disaster. *International Journal of Emergency Mental Health, 5,* 211-215.

Centers for Disease Control and Prevention. (2002). Deaths in World Trade Center terrorist attacks—New York City, 2001. *Mortality and Morbidity Weekly Report, 51(Special Issue),* 16-18.

Cohen, J. & Cohen, P. (1983). *Applied multiple regression/correlation analysis for the behavioral sciences* (2nd ed.). Hillsdale, NJ: Lawrence Erlbaum.

Derogatis, L. R. (2001). *Brief Symptom Inventory 18 (BSI-18) manual.* Minnetonka, MN: NCS Assessments.

Everly, G. S., Flannery, R. B., & Mitchell, J. T. (2000). Critical incident stress management (CISM): A review of the literature. *Aggression and Violent Behavior, 5,* 23-40.

Flannery, R. B., & Everly, G. S. (2000). Crisis intervention: A review. *International Journal of Emergency Mental Health, 2,* 119-125.

Flannery, R. B., & Everly, G. S. (2004). Critical incident stress management (CISM): Updated review of findings, 1998-2002. *Aggression and Violent Behavior, 9,* 319-329.

Freedy, J. R., Kilpatrick, D. G., & Resnick, H. S. (1993). Natural disasters and mental health: Theory, assessment, and intervention. *Journal of Social Behavior and Personality, [Special Issue] 8,* 49-103.

Galea, S., Ahern, J., Resnick, H., Kilpatrick, D., Bucuvalas, M., Gold, J., et al. (2002). Psychological sequelae of the September 11 terrorist attacks in New York City. *The New England Journal of Medicine, 346,* 982-987.

Galea, S., Vlahov, D., Resnick, H., Ahern, J., Susser, E., Gold, J., et al. (2003). Trends in probable posttraumatic stress in New York City after the September 11 terrorist attacks. *American Journal of Epidemiology, 158,* 514-524.

Gleser, G. C., Green, B. L., & Winget, C. (1981). *Prolonged psychosocial effects of disaster: A study of Buffalo Creek.* New York: Academic Press.

Green, B. L. (1991). Evaluating the effects of disasters. *Psychological Assessment, 3,* 538-546.

Grieger, T. A., Fullerton, C. S., & Ursano, R. J. (2003). Posttraumatic stress disorder, alcohol use, and perceived safety after the terrorist attack on the Pentagon. *Psychiatric Services, 54,* 1380-1382.

Groves, R. M., Fowler, F. J., Couper, M. P., Lepkowski, J. M., Singer, E., & Tourangeau, R. (2004). *Survey methodology.* New York: Wiley.

Hokanson, M. & Wirth, B. (2000). The critical incident stress debriefing process for the Los Angeles County Fire Department: Automatic and effective. *International Journal of Emergency Mental Health, 2,* 249-257.

Hulley, S. B., Cummings, S. R., Browner, W. S., Grady, D., Hearst, N., & Newman, T. B. (2001). *Designing clinical research: An epidemiological approach* (2nd ed.). New York: Lippincott.

Kaplan, Z., Iancu, I., & Bodner, E. (2001). A review of psychological debriefing after extreme stress. *Psychiatric Services, 52,* 824-827.

Kessler, R. C., Little, R. J., & Groves, R. M. (1995). Advances in strategies for minimizing and adjusting for survey nonresponse. *Epidemiologic Reviews, 17,* 192-204.

Kilpatrick, D. G., Resnick, H., Freedy, J. R., Pelcovitz, D., Resnick, P., Roth, S., et al. (1998). The posttraumatic stress disorder field trial: Evaluation of the PTSD construct—criteria A through E. In T. A. Widiger, A. J. Frances, H. A. Pincus, R. Ross, M. B. First, W. Davis, & M. Kline. (Eds.), *DSM-IV Sourcebook—Vol. 4* (pp. 803-844). Washington, DC: American Psychiatric Association.

Kilpatrick, D. G., Ruggiero, K. J., Acierno, R., Saunders, B. E., Resnick, H. S., & Best, C. L. (2003). Violence and risk of PTSD, major depression, substance abuse/dependence, and comorbidity: Results from the national survey of adolescents. *Journal of Consulting and Clinical Psychology, 71,* 692-700.

King, M. (1986). At risk drinking among general practice attenders: Validation of the CAGE questionnaire. *Psychological Medicine, 16,* 213-217.

Jacobs, J., Horne-Moyer, H. L., & Jones, R. (2004). The effectiveness of critical incident stress debriefing with primary and secondary trauma victims. *International Journal of Emergency Mental Health, 6,* 5-14.

Luna, J. T. (2002). Collaborative assessment and healing in schools after large-scale terrorist attacks. *International Journal of Emergency Mental Health, 4,* 201-208.

Magruder-Habib, K., Stevens, H. A., & Alling, W. C. (1993). Relative performance of the MAST, VAST, and CAGE versus DSM-III-R criteria for alcohol dependence. *Journal of Clinical Epidemiology, 46,* 435-441.

Mitchell, J. T. (2003). Major misconceptions in crisis intervention. *International Journal of Emergency Mental Health, 5,* 185-197.

Mitchell, J. T. (2004). Characteristics of successful early intervention programs. *International Journal of Emergency Mental Health, 6,* 175-184.

Neter, J., Wasserman, W., & Kutner, M. H. (1990). *Applied linear statistical models* (3rd ed.). Homewood, IL: Irwin.

Noji, E. K. (1997). The nature of disaster: General characteristics and public health effects. In E. K. Noji (Ed.), *The public health consequences of disasters* (pp. 3-20). New York: Oxford University Press.

Norris, F. H. (1992). Epidemiology of trauma: Frequency and impact of different potentially traumatic events on different demographic groups. *Journal of Consulting and Clinical Psychology, 60,* 409-418.

North, C. S., Nixon, S. J., Shariat, S., Mallonee, S., McMillen, J. C., Spitznagel, E. L., et al. (1999). Psychiatric disorders among survivors of the Oklahoma City bombing. *Journal of the American Medical Association, 282,* 755-762.

Ortega, A. N., Rosenheck, R., Alegria, M., & Desai, R. A. (2000). Acculturation and lifetime risk of psychiatric and substance use disorders among Hispanics. *The Journal of Nervous and Mental Disease, 188,* 728-735.

Pfefferbaum, B. & Doughty, D. E. (2001). Increased alcohol use in a treatment sample of Oklahoma City bombing victims. *Psychiatry, 64,* 296-303.

Resnick, H. S., Kilpatrick, D. G., Dansky, B. S., Saunders, B. E., & Best, C. (1993). Prevalence of civilian trauma and posttraumatic stress disorder in a representative national sample of women. *Journal of Consulting and Clinical Psychology, 61,* 984-991.

Rosenberg, M. (1979). *Conceiving the self.* New York: Basic Books.

Rubonis, A. V. & Bickman, L. (1991). Psychological impairment in the wake of disaster: The disaster- psychopathology relationship. *Psychology Bulletin, 109,* 384-399.

Sherbourne, C. D. & Stewart, A. L. (1991). The MOS social support survey. *Social Science in Medicine, 32,* 705-714.

Spitzer, R. L., Williams, J. B., & Gibbon, M. (1987). *Structured clinical interview for DSM-III-R–Non-patient version.* New York: Biometrics Research Department, New York State Psychiatric Institute.

Stata Corporation. (2001). Stata, version 7. 0. [Computer software]. College Station, TX: Stata Corporation.

Vlahov, D., Galea, S., Ahern, J., Resnick, H., Boscarino, J. A., Gold, J., et al. (2004). Consumption of cigarettes, alcohol, and marijuana among New York City residents six months after the September 11 terrorist attacks. *American Journal of Drug and Alcohol Abuse, 30,* 385-407.

Vlahov, D., Galea, S., Ahern, J., Resnick, H., & Kilpatrick, D. (2004). Sustained increased consumption of cigarettes, alcohol, and marijuana among Manhattan residents after September 11, 2001. *American Journal of Public Health, 94,* 253-254.

International Journal of Emergency Mental Health, Vol. 6, No. 4, pp. 185-196 © 2004 Chevron Publishing ISSN 1522-4821

Economic Evaluation of CISM – A Pilot Study

Joachim Vogt
University of Copenhagen

Jörg Leonhardt
German Air Traffic Control

Birgit Köper
Federal Institute for Occupational Safety and Health

Stefan Pennig
Leadership Performance Consulting

ABSTRACT: *This paper reports the implementation of the Critical Incident Stress Management (CISM) Program with the German Air Traffic Control Services (DFS). Particular attention is paid to the application of CISM services to a population of air traffic controllers. An extended economic efficiency evaluation was conducted for the European Organization for the Safety of Air Navigation (Eurocontrol) Brussels. Questionnaires and interviews were obtained from forty-seven air traffic controllers (ATCOs), thirteen CISM peers, and the program manager. The collected data describe the goals of the program and their achievement, program implementation, costs, and benefits. The results revealed that after five years the program's estimated fiscal benefits had exceeded the costs (break-even). Moreover, it had improved the safety culture within DFS in many ways. For this reason, controllers who never consulted a peer reported many benefits of the program. They believed that having the program was a good idea as a back-up support in case they would ever need it. [International Journal of Emergency Medical Health, 2004 6(4),pp. 185-196].*

KEY WORDS: Air traffic controllers, Critical Incident Stress Management, CISM, critical incidents, critical incident stress, cost-benefit-analysis, economic evaluation, efficiency, return on investment

Joachim Vogt, Ph.D., Dipl., Department of Psychology, University of Copenhagen, Denmark; **Jörg Leonhardt, M.S.W., Dipl.,** German Air Traffic Control, Langen, Germany; **Birgit Köper, Ph.D., Dipl.** Federal Institute for Occupational Safety and Health (FIOSH), Dortmund, Germany; **Stefan Pennig, Dipl.,** Leadership Performance Consulting, Essen, Germany. This research was financed by the European Organization for the Safety of Air Navigation (Eurocontrol), Rue de la Fusée 96, B-1130 Brussels. The authors would like to thank all DFS staff who contributed to the study and three anonymous reviewers for comments on an earlier version of this paper. Special thanks are due to Shannon G. Mitchell, Ph.D., Research Associate, Johns Hopkins University, Bloomberg School of Public Health, Department of Heath Policy and Management for her valuable and detailed feedback during the revision of the manuscript. Correspondence concerning this article should be addressed to Joachim Vogt, University of Copenhagen, Department of Psychology, Njalsgade 88, DK-2300 Copenhagen S. Email: joachim.vogt @psy.ku.dk

Introduction

The German Air Traffic Control Services (Deutsche Flugsicherung GmbH, DFS) is responsible for the safe and expeditious coordination of air traffic in Germany. Since 1993 the DFS has been a private enterprise; it works at seventeen centers throughout Germany. The two major divisions are (a) the radar centers for en-route control and (b) the air traffic control towers responsible for aircraft taking off or landing at German airports. At the time the study was conducted, 1700 air traffic controllers worked for DFS.

For several years, German air traffic controllers had sought information from their supervisors about how their reactions to a critical incident might be managed. Supervisors and managers, on the other hand, were interested in programs that could provide support during a crisis and enhance the coping abilities of air traffic controllers (ATCOs). Beginning in 1998, DFS researched appropriate methods to intervene with employees who experienced critical incident stress. Among the many documents on the issue of staff crisis support that were reviewed during the research period were two that were published by Eurocontrol, the European Organization for the Safety of Air Navigation. Eurocontrol's published papers on crisis support programs for air traffic control personnel had considerable influence on the DFS decision to establish a Critical Incident Stress Management (CISM) program in accordance with the standards of the International Critical Incident Stress Foundation (ICISF) (Everly, 1999, 2000; Everly & Mitchell, 1997; Mitchell & Everly, 2001; Woldring, 1996; Woldring & Amat, 1997).

Air Traffic Controllers and CISM

Air traffic controllers are selected and trained to have high stress resistance, to work in a team, and to possess individual decision-making abilities. An ATCO must be able to maintain composure and to make optimal decisions in difficult situations that place aircraft, crews, and passengers in jeopardy. Controllers need to rely on themselves and on their team.

ATCOs maintain a safe distance (e.g., five nautical miles) between en-route aircraft. That safe distance may vary depending on the airspace, the type of aircraft, and the overall operation. A separation loss between two aircraft (the horizontal distance between aircraft drops below five nautical miles–say 4.8 miles) even if not considered critical by pilots, cabin crew, passengers, or the public is an existential threat to the ATCO's view of his or her professional performance. Although a separation loss usually does not lead to an accident, it can cause considerable stress reactions for the controller(s) involved in the incident.

ATCOs had historically been reluctant to approach mental health professionals with their stress problems. Additionally, they were hesitant to discuss their stress reactions with people outside of their profession. Specially trained ATCO personnel were in a unique position to offer support to their colleagues. It was hoped that a peer-based CISM program, with mental health services backup when necessary, would be more acceptable to ATCOs. These considerations led to the development of the peer support CISM system for DFS.

Stress Reaction in ATCOs

Stress literature is replete with long lists of cognitive, physical, emotional, and behavioral signs and symptoms (Ev-

erly and Mitchell, 1997; Flannery, 1998; Mitchell and Everly, 2001). Repetition of the wide range of human stress reactions here would not serve the primary purposes of this article. It should suffice to state that significant stress reactions can seriously impact the crucial work of air traffic controllers. Stress reactions may impair work performance in the following ways:

- ☐ Decision-making problems
- ☐ Concentration problems
- ☐ Problems in identifying known persons or objects (aircraft)
- ☐ Impaired memory
- ☐ Indecisiveness
- ☐ Confusion

Self-doubts and a feeling of abnormality may be the performance-crippling and sometimes career-threatening consequences of stress reactions for the ATCO.

DFS CISM Program Objectives

The first objective of a successful coping strategy is *stabilization* during the acute phases of the crisis reactions and a return to normalcy. The second aim is a *rapid and sustainable re-establishment of personal abilities and fitness for work*. The DFS peer support CISM program attempts to achieve these two strategic objectives by reducing the impact of a stressful event, by facilitating an employee's return to work, and by educating the staff about the signs and symptoms of traumatic stress as well as the appropriate mechanisms to manage that stress. In addition, the program attempts to identify, as early as practical, staff members who may need additional support or professional referrals to recover fully. Restoring the ability to work is important in the coping process for the individual, but there may be economic advantages as well. The investigation of the economic advantages was the primary purpose for this study.

System-wide CISM Program Orientation

In 1998, after consultation with managers and air traffic controllers, the decision was made to introduce CISM in the DFS. An information campaign involved managers, employees, and operational personnel for DFS functions. Broad acceptance and support of the program was paramount. Workshops, presentations, briefings, and other internal media ensured that DFS employees were informed about the program. A special training program entitled "CISM for Supervisors" was offered to operations room supervisory personnel.

Selection and Qualification of the Peers

In order to achieve maximum trust and confidentiality, the controllers voted on colleagues to become peers. It was important that the controllers have confidence in the peers with respect to their personal skills and their integrity. The elected peers were informed about their potential future tasks and the expectations placed upon them. They were then given the option to accept the vote and to take part in the CISM courses or to refuse. All elected peers accepted the vote and participated in the qualification training.

Peer Training

A minimum of five peers per radar center and two peers per tower were designated. Altogether, 65 peers were elected and went through the following training courses:

- CISM Group Crisis Intervention
- CISM Individual Crisis Intervention and Peer Support
- CISM Advanced tactics

All courses were consistent with ICISF standards and, upon completion of training, peers received ICISF certificates. The CISM Individual Crisis Intervention and Advanced tactics courses were taught by Jeffrey T. Mitchell, Ph.D., the developer of the CISM model. The peer debriefings and psychological supervision after crisis intervention services are conducted by a team facilitated by Jörg Leonhardt, the DFS CISM manager.

In an effort to maintain the health of the peer support personnel and to keep them informed of developments in CISM, special supervision meetings are held annually in each tower unit and radar center. Additionally any peer may request a supervision meeting at any time. The CISM Forum, a conference of all DFS peers, is held once a year at the DFS headquarters. Through these supervision meetings and continuing education, the peers are supported and the quality of their work is maintained.

Status 2004

Since its introduction, anecdotal reports indicate that the DFS CISM program is perceived as a value by DFS employees. The service is accepted by managers and controllers alike. Even top management personnel have voiced their support of the CISM program. Their common understanding of the program itself as well as their experience of the program's objectives appear to promote a workplace atmosphere of mutual support. The number of trained peers has expanded to 75. The peers at the respective DFS units regularly inform operations room supervisors about the program

and introduce trainees to CISM concepts. International cooperation with other European air navigation service providers and with Eurocontrol is well established. Regular exchanges of information and training opportunities are common. ICISF and DFS are cooperating and demonstrating a strong and productive partnership.

Business Benefits

In an effort to assess and document the business benefits of a CISM program, DFS volunteered to participate in a Eurocontrol feasibility study on the applicability of economic evaluation methods to human resource programs. The key findings from the study will be presented in the results section of this paper. In the following section, the economic evaluation models used in the study are introduced. The combination of human resource evaluation and utility analysis was the theoretical basis on which the study instruments were developed.

Human Resource Program Evaluation

The theoretical model underlying the economic evaluation method used in this study is the Human Resources Evaluation Model (Kirkpatrick, 1994; Phillips, 1996). It was originally conceived to classify and determine the effects of staff trainings. The original model consists of four levels:

1. Reaction. Describes the satisfaction of participants with the training (content, method, organizational framework, behavior of the trainer, etc.). For this study, this level was obtained by asking the peers to evaluate their CISM courses and asking the controllers about their reactions to consulting a peer.

2. Learning. Refers to the learning effects of the training, independent of whether they are practically applied. This level was obtained by asking the peers about the knowledge, abilities, and attitudes they obtained during the CISM courses and asking the controllers what they learned from consulting a peer.

3. Behavior. Comprises behavioral changes on the job, which indicate the transfer and adoption of learning effects in the work situation. In this study, the peers were asked to what extent the CISM qualification prepared them for their service and in what respect it changed their behavior during a consultation. The controllers were asked to what extent consulting a peer helped them to return to work.

4. Results. Measures the resulting effects of behavioral changes (as relevant for the organization).

These include

□ product quality

□ efficiency of performance

□ client satisfaction

□ image

□ staff satisfaction, fluctuation, and absenteeism

□ cost reduction

In this study, the impairment of essential ATCO skills after the critical incident was assessed to determine what factors changed in demand characteristics in the person-task interaction. The study also assessed how the impairments were overcome.

Phillips (1996) added another level to the model, which in the framework of this study is labeled

5. Impact: Evaluates the profitability of the training (return on investment: ROI), which is measured in monetary units. The full cost of training is estimated together with the turn-off (ROI = [revenue – costs] / costs). In this study, the return on investment of CISM was measured as the estimated cost reduction by gained controller days due to accelerated return to work relative to the full costs of the program per controller. This final step is the core of utility analysis (Boudreau & Ramstad, 2003), while the previous steps belong to the human resource evaluation

Method

Participants

Three radar centers were selected for the data gathering: Bremen, Munich, and Karlsruhe. Three peers volunteered for a face-to-face interview in Bremen, six in Munich, and four in Karlsruhe. After the interview, the peers were asked to distribute questionnaires among controllers who had consulted a peer after a critical incident ("CISM-group") and among colleagues who did not ("non-CISM-group"). A total of 47 controller questionnaires and 13 peer interviews comprised the data basis for the study. Moreover, the manager who introduced the CISM program in the DFS was interviewed, especially with respect to the implementation and costs of the program.

The controllers were between 20 and 55 years of age with the majority in their late thirties. Six of the 13 peers were also in their late thirties, and no one was younger than 30. The age distribution differed between groups, with the CISM-group comprising both younger and older controllers than the non-CISM-group. The central age tendency in both groups was again late thirties. The gender distribution was balanced in all groups and representative for DFS controllers. Among the 13 peers were 10 males and three females, among the 47 controllers were 37 males and 10 females. The respective numbers in the CISM-group were 15 and three and in the non-CISM-group 16 and four. Four controllers reported on a critical incident before 1999 and were excluded from the analysis. Another five controllers did not describe a critical incident and/or did not answer the question whether they had a CISM intervention or not and had to be excluded as well.

It is important to note that the data collection at Karlsruhe was different in some respects from the other two centers because it was affected by the Überlingen accident, This mid-air collision happened on July 1, 2002, near Überlingen, Lake Constance, Germany, at 21:35:32 (Universal Time Code). A Tupolev TU 154M, which was on a flight from Moscow, Russia, to Barcelona, Spain, and a Boeing B757-200, on a flight from Bergamo, Italy, to Brussels, Belgium, collided at a flight level of about 35,000 ft. There were a total of 71 people (mostly children) on board the two aircrafts; none survived. The two aircraft were under the control of the Swiss air traffic service provider (Swisscontrol). However, the accident also affected many controllers in Karlsruhe who saw the catastrophe coming on their radar screens and tried to warn their Swiss colleagues. Two Karlsruhe peers were members of the CISM team sent to Switzerland to treat the Swisscontrol employees. The Lake Constance mid-air collision had a great impact in Karlsruhe and probably required more utilization of CISM than the other centers. This is probably one reason for the high commitment of Karlsruhe controllers to the program and the evaluation study (this center accounted for 26 of 47 returned questionnaires).

Design and Procedure

The peers were asked to distribute 100 questionnaires among the controllers. They were instructed to spread them widely with regard to the demographic characteristics of the controllers and the types and number of critical incidents they had experienced. Moreover, they included controllers who had a CISM intervention after a critical incident ("CISM-group") and those who had not ("non-CISM-group"). Both groups used the same questionnaire, which included an item asking them to describe a critical incident they experienced and the factors that contributed to their recovery. The CISM-group additionally reported on their experience with the CISM intervention.

It was expected that both groups were different in many respects (see hypotheses). Therefore, controllers who did not request CISM were not considered a control group for CISM effects. The fiscal benefits of the program are estimated within the CISM-group only.

Questionnaire and Interview Structure

Thirteen peers volunteered for an interview and 47 controllers returned their questionnaires. Both study instruments considered the interactions of peers and controllers regarding reaction, learning, behavior, and respective results as well as economic impact according to the underlying theoretical model derived from combining human resource evaluation with utility analysis.

Open and scaled questions were used in the interview with peers and the questionnaire for ATCOs. Open questions, concerning for example the perceived aims of the CISM program, were, post hoc, categorized into clusters of similar answers. This was done independently by two coding experts with an inter-rater agreement above 34%, which is considered satisfactory. Most scaled questions, for example the grade of goal achievement of the CISM program, were obtained with a German 5-point scale according to Rohrmann (1978). Rohrmann suggested the five steps of the scale be equally distant and normal distributed, which allows for statistical operations like averaging or significance testing. Although the nature of the study is exploratory, some of the differences within and between groups were tested statistically.

Apart from questions to be answered in Rohrmann steps, percentages, days (e.g., of illness and recovery), or other units, the questionnaire also contained items derived from standard questionnaires:

1. Ability requirements which are defined in the Fleishman Job Analysis Survey (Fleishman & Reilly, 1992) and play an important role in the selection process of German ATCOs (Deuchert & Eißfeld, 1998). The study subjects were asked to what extent, in Rohrmann steps, task requirements like originality (the ability to develop solutions when standards are not applicable), problem sensitivity, perceptual speed, selective attention, multi-tasking, motivation, self-awareness, and stress resistance were impaired after the critical incident.

2. Psychosomatic ailments, which are used, for example, in the Gießener Beschwerdebogen (Brähler & Scheer, 1983) and in the ICISF symptom checklist. Symptoms like

drowsiness, intrusive memories, anxiety, flashbacks, emotions of guilt, and the occurrence of nightmares were rated on a five point scale from "did not occur" to "occurred strongly" after the incident.

We believed that those ATCOs requesting CISM after an incident did so because they perceived more impaired abilities and psychosomatic symptoms than colleagues who chose no CISM service. Therefore, they would also need more time for recovery. For this reason we hypothesized that CISM would contribute significantly more to their recovery than other factors within group. The two main hypotheses concern (a) comparisons between the two groups and (b) the recovery and accelerated return to work within the CISM-group.

Hypothesis 1a: The CISM-group reports to have had higher impairment of work abilities (e.g., originality, problem sensitivity, perceptual speed, selective attention, multi-tasking, self-awareness, stress resistance) after the critical incident than the non-CISM-group.

Hypothesis 1b: The CISM-group reports to have had more intense psychosomatic symptoms (drowsiness, intrusive memories, anxiety, flashbacks, emotions of guilt, nightmares) after the critical incident than the non-CISM-group.

Hypothesis 1c: The CISM-group reports to have had needed more days to fully recover after a critical incident than the non-CISM-group.

Hypothesis 2a: Within the CISM-group, controllers attribute more of their recovery to CISM than to other factors.

Hypothesis 2b: Within the CISM-group, the estimated savings on the basis of accelerated return to work will exceed the implementation and maintenance costs.

Hypotheses 1a, 1b, 1c, and 2a were tested by t-tests. Within each hypothesis, the alpha error probability is set at 0.05 and, in case of hypotheses 1a and 1b, corrected for multiple tests according to Holm (Krauth, 1988).

Results

Temporary Ability Impairment and Psychosomatic Complaints

As shown in Table 1, the CISM-group reported greater temporary impairment of abilities such as stress resistance, self-awareness, and multi-tasking. After alpha error correction, only the difference concerning stress resistance remains statistically significant and supports hypothesis 1a (p = 0.003). Stress resistance was repeatedly reported to be the most important requirement in air traffic control (Kastner, Vogt,

Table 1.
Mean Self-Reported Impairment of Abilities by Group

Abilities	N	Mean	SE	t[1]	DF	p[1]
Originality						
CISM	19	2.1	0.29	0.02	35	0.494
Non-CISM	18	2.1	0.25			
Problem Solving						
CISM	19	2.2	0.29	0.41	33	0.339
Non-CISM	16	2.0	0.24			
Perceptual Speed						
CISM	19	2.5	0.28	1.89	35	0.033
Non-CISM	18	1.8	0.19			
Selective Attention						
CISM	19	2.5	0.29	1.23	35	0.114
Non-CISM	18	2.1	0.25			
Multi-Tasking						
CISM	18	2.7	0.27	2.21	34	0.017
Non-CISM	18	1.9	0.23			
Motivation						
CISM	18	2.3	0.27	0.96	34	0.171
Non-CISM	18	1.9	0.22			
Self-Awareness						
CISM	18	2.9	0.29	2.13	34	0.020
Non-CISM	18	2.1	0.25			
Stress Resistance						
CISM	18	3.1	0.26	2.92	34	0.003*
Non-CISM	18	2.1	0.22			

[1] one-tailed
* significant at the 0.05 level

Köper, Udovic & Hagemann, 2000; Kastner, Köper, Hagemann & Hein, 2002). Table 2 shows the level of psychosomatic symptoms experienced in both groups. Again, the CISM-group tended to report slightly more intense reactions than the non-CISM-group. The occurrence of flashbacks and nightmares tended to have been experienced somewhat stronger in controllers who requested a CISM intervention. However, these results were not statistically significant from the non-CISM-group and hypothesis 1b could not be accepted.

Economic Benefits

The controllers were asked to describe the course of their performance recovery after the incident. With the aid of a diagram, they were instructed to divide the time between the critical incident and full recovery into four equal time intervals T1-T4. Then they rated their working performance for T0 (directly after the critical incident), T1, T2, and T3. By definition, performance at T4 was 100%. Connecting the ratings displayed an approximation of the course of recovery.

Figure 1 displays the average self-reported performance recovery for the controllers who requested CISM after T0 (CISM-group) and those who did not (non-CISM-group). As already demonstrated for the impairment of working skills and psychosomatic symptoms, the CISM-group reported greater adverse impacts on work performance than the non-CISM-group directly after the critical incident (T0, starting point of the curves). The reason for this might be that people who admit a suboptimal performance after an incident and

Table 2.
Mean Self-Reported Impairment of Psychosomatic Symptoms by Group

Symptoms	CISM			Non-CISM			t[1]	df	p[1]
	M	SE	n	M	SE	n			
Drowsiness	2.2	0.34	19	2.1	0.25	18	0.37	35	0.359
Intrusive Thoughts	3.0	0.31	20	2.4	0.29	18	1.30	36	0.101
Anxiety	2.4	0.38	18	2.1	0.25	18	0.73	34	0.236
Flashbacks	2.7	0.28	20	1.8	0.22	18	2.38	36	0.012
Guilt	2.5	0.31	20	1.9	0.27	18	1.33	36	0.097
Nightmares	1.9	0.26	20	1.2	0.13	18	2.25	36	0.016

[1] one-tailed

then seek treatment are different from those who do not. Moreover, it is possible that the CISM-group had critical incidents of greater intensity than the non-CISM-group. However, the recovery of the CISM-group from this baseline proceeded much faster than the recovery of the non-CISM-group (slope of the curves in Figure 1).

The self-reported recovery process in both groups depended on the kind of incident, as shown in Table 3. Both groups needed more days to recover fully when exposed to an accident. Although the critical incidents, which were described in an open section of the questionnaire, did not differ in severity, the controllers who requested CISM reported a longer recovery period and therefore were obviously more affected. The average duration until total recovery after the Überlingen accident was 12 days in the CISM-group and 3 days in the non-CISM-group. The durations to recover from a critical incident like a separation loss were 4 and 1 day(s), respectively for the two groups. The CISM-group needed statistically significant more days to recover from a critical incident than the non-CISM-group (p = 0.015), thus supporting hypothesis 1c.

Although the subjects who had requested CISM also had more room to change from the lower baseline, they traced the largest part of their recovery back to the organized, structured, and professional help provided by CISM (Table 4). The CISM-group ascribed more than one-third of their recovery to the CISM consultation. The difference to the next largest contributor (spontaneous recovery, 26%) tended to support hypothesis 2a but did not reach statistical significance (t = 1.44, df = 32, p = 0.08). In the non-CISM-group, spontaneous recovery and support of colleagues were reported to have the largest impact on recovery. Interestingly, even in this group a small amount of recovery was attributed to CISM. The interviewed peers reported that the mere fact of being available is appreciated by the ATCOs as providing support.

Since both groups have significantly different starting points, a comparison was hardly possible. Instead, the benefit of CISM was calculated within the CISM-group. The CISM-group reported the following contributions of CISM to their recovery in percent:

☐ 35% after the accident of Überlingen
☐ 32% after critical incidents (mainly separation losses)
☐ 65% after personal incidents.

Although CISM seemed especially effective after personal (private) incidents, it is important to note that there

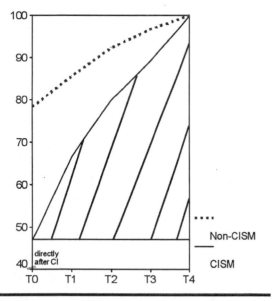

Figure 1: Average self-reported performance (in percent of full work capacity) of controllers who requested CISM directly after the incident (T0) compared to those who did not. The hatched area marks the performance improvement, which was attributed to CISM by 36 percent.

Table 3.
Self-reported Days Needed to Full Recovery After a Critical Event (Days)

		Überlingen Incident	Other Critical Incidents (mainly separation losses)	Personal Incident
CISM	M	11.9	4.3	0.3
	SE	[1]	1.21	[1]
	n	[1]	15	[1]
Non-CISM	M	3.3	1.1	—
	SE	[1]	0.52	[1]
	n	[1]	13	[1]
	t	[1]	2.28	[1]
	df	[1]	26	[1]
	p	[1]	0.015*	[1]

[1] Cells remain empty because the numbers of cases were too small for statistical testing.
* significant at the 0.05 level

were just three cases and they reported only minor impairment. Critical work-related incidents, such as separation loss, were reported more frequently, and the Überlingen accident had an outstanding impact.

Combining Figure 1 and the reported contribution of CISM to percentage of recovery allows for the calculation of monetary effects of CISM in the unit of gained controller days. For this purpose, the performance recovery curve (Figure 1) was taken for each individual controller. For each CISM-subject, the integrated performance improvement (hatched area, Figure 1) was multiplied by the percentage contribution of CISM to the recovery and the sum of total recovery days. Thus, the business benefit of CISM in gained controller days was estimated to

- 2.9 days after the accident of Überlingen
- 1.3 days after critical incidents (mainly separation losses)
- 0.1 day after personal incidents

This illustrates that in the case of the Überlingen accident, CISM was on average associated with a self-reported acceleration of recovery of 3 days and after critical incidents, for example a separation loss, it was associated with a reported acceleration recovery rate of 1 day.

With respect to the number of gained controller days (1 for each controller involved in a separation loss and 3 for each controller who experienced the Überlingen accident), the economic effects of CISM in the study sample were calculated as follows.

In our sample, 32 controllers described separation losses and five had experienced the accident of Überlingen. The CISM-related improved recovery cumulates to

$$32 * 1 \text{ day} + 5 * 3 \text{ days} = 47 \text{ days } (1)$$

The DFS calculates the average full-costs for a controller day to be 840 Euros; therefore, the costs of one controller day were set at

$$1 \text{ controller day} = 958 \text{ USD } (2)$$

(For the conversion of Euro to USD the rate 1:1.14 was used which was valid at the time of this calculation on September 30, 2003.)

The monetary benefits of the CISM program only with respect to our sample then were

$$47 \text{ days} * 958 \text{ USD} = 45,026 \text{ USD } (3)$$

The total DFS CISM program since 1999 cost about 400,000 Euros, converted to USD gave the

$$\text{full cost of DFS CISM} = 456,000 \text{ USD } (4)$$

Since there were 1700 active controllers in Germany at the time of the study in 2003, this makes

$$456,000 \text{ USD} / 1700 \text{ controllers} = 268 \text{ USD costs per controller } (5)$$

to install and maintain the DFS CISM program during the five years between implementation and evaluation study.

For our sample of 47 controllers, therefore, CISM cost

$$47 \text{ controllers} * 268 \text{ USD} = 12,596 \text{ USD } (6)$$

The total cost reduction due to CISM in our sample as the difference of costs (6) and benefits (3) results in

Table 4.

Mean Percentage Contribution of Several Factors to Full Recovery Following an Incident[1]

		CISM	Spontaneous Recovery	Colleagues	Individuals outside DFS	Vacancies	SPA[2]
CISM	M	36	26	23	19	8	10
	SE	4.11	5.98	3.88	4.07	4.41	10
	n	20	14	17	14	3	2
Non-CISM	M	3	45	35	27	12	15
	SE	2.86	8.63	6.38	7.52	9.28	15
	n	7	14	12	12	3	2
	t[3]	4.51	1.80	1.73	0.98	0.32	0.28
	df	25	26	27	24	4	2
	p[3]	0.000*	0.042	0.048	0.168	0.381	0.404

[1] Subjects were instructed that the sum of all percentages had to be one hundred percent. One subject was excluded from analysis because this instruction was not followed. Other factors that were rated with a percentage but not specified are not shown in the table. The mean percentage can exceed one hundred percent because it is averaged between subjects.

[2] The word derives from a Belgian town whose springs reputedly had curative powers. It is used throughout Europe to summarize treatments including mineral and/or thermal springs, massages, and other alternative medical treatments.

[3] one-tailed

* significant at the 0.05 level

$$45{,}026\,USD - 12{,}596\,USD = 32{,}430\,USD \quad (7)$$

The return on investment ROI as cost reduction (7) relative to investment (6) within the study sample and calculated in percent comes to

$$ROI = 32{,}430\,USD / 12{,}596\,USD * 100 = 257\% \quad (8)$$

As expected in hypothesis 2b, the DFS CISM program's estimated fiscal benefits had thereby exceeded the costs already in 2003.

Additional Benefits

Controllers and peers were asked to assess whether CISM was worthwhile for themselves and for DFS. Eighty-three percent of the peers reported that CISM was extremely worthwhile for their personal development. Seventy percent of the CISM-group also rated the benefit for themselves as extremely high. Intriguing is the finding that the majority of the non-CISM-group also perceived benefits of CISM. Again, it seems that the option to consult a peer may be immensely useful. The benefits for DFS were rated extremely high by 69 to 75% of controllers and peers (Table 5). Even the majority of those controllers who never consulted a peer answered in the same

direction. As mentioned above, the mere presence of peers and the opportunity to consult them seems to be effective, even if this opportunity was never used.

When asked to describe the quality of improvements in the DFS through CISM, one-third of the peers mentioned an improvement in the way failures are handled (error culture). In their view, the implementation of CISM helped to overcome the last remains of a blame culture and to develop an open culture of trust that supports learning from errors (Angenendt, 2003). The controllers of both groups placed the peers' consulting into the foreground and labeled it "professional supervision" (Table 6). Whereas the majority of controllers pronounced this supervision as a chance to talk, the peers emphasized the prevention of long-term emotional consequences as a CISM aim. The goals that were reported for the DFS CISM program were rated very well achieved (Table 7).

Discussion

The individually experienced impact of a critical incident is decisive for requesting CISM services. An accident like the mid-air collision over Überlingen, however, makes the

Table 5.
Additional benefits of CISM in the view of peers and controllers who requested CISM after a critical incident compared to those who did not

		Not At All	Slightly	Moderately	Very	Extremely
Perceived Benefit of CISM for Oneself (Percent)	CISM	—	5.0	15.0	10.0	70.0
	Non-CISM	11.8	17.6	5.9	23.5	41.2
	Peer	8.3	—	—	8.3	83.3
Perceived Benefit of CISM for DFS (Percent)	CISM	—	5.6	5.6	16.7	72.2
	Non-CISM	—	6.3	6.3	18.8	68.8
	Peer	—	—	8.3	16.7	75.0

advantages of peer support most obvious. The experience also depends on the coping abilities of the individual, which largely determine the impact on well-being and performance. The results showed that not every controller requested CISM after a critical incident. In these cases their own personal resources were likely considered sufficient coping strategies. Only serious incidents that exceed the personal coping capabilities of most people may result in widespread participation in CISM.

Positive Effects

CISM reduced the time off for individuals who consulted a peer after a critical incident. After accidents, this decrease of recovery need was on average 3 days; after critical incidents, it was 1 day. Thus, CISM had a considerable economic benefit. It led to an estimated cost reduction of approximately 32,430 USD in the investigated sample which—considering the total costs for CISM in the years 1999-2003—accorded to a conservative approximation of 257% return on investment. This success is likely underestimated, since the actual time

of recovery after an accident or severe critical incident may be longer than the controllers admitted in the questionnaire. As some of the peers acknowledged, there still is a mentality among ATCOs that makes them expect and perceive overall personal control.

From these results, one can conclude that the influence of adverse emotional effects on performance is high. The comparison between the CISM- and non-CISM-groups showed that the experienced impact of the critical incident in terms of impaired working ability and psychosomatic complaints was higher in the CISM-group. The starting point in the recovery process of the controllers who requested CISM was lower than in the non-CISM-group. Directly after the incident, the CISM-group reported a loss of performance capability of 52%; the non-CISM-group estimated 21% (Figure 1).

Besides the accelerated recovery which can be expressed in monetary values, the controllers and peers mentioned additional benefits. Additional benefits were also reported by Flannery (1998) who found that the Assaulted Staff Action

Table 6.
Quality of Improvements in the DFS through CISM (Percent)

	Willingness to talk	Professional Supervision	Error Culture	Open-Mindedness	Acceptance of Emotions	Fit for Work	No Improvements
CISM	—	46.7	6.7	6.7	20.0	13.3	6.7
Non-CISM	7.1	42.9	28.6	—	7.1	7.1	7.1
Peer	16.7	8.3	33.3	16.7	8.3	—	16.7

Table 7.

Perceived goals and perceived goal achievement of CISM in the DFS

		Supervision	Coping	Consulting	Prevention	Fit for Work	Communication Culture	Other
Perceived Goals in percent (multiple answers were allowed)	CISM	65.0	—	20.0	35.0	5.0	25.0	55.0
	Non-CISM	77.8	16.7	11.1	16.7	22.2	22.2	27.8
	Peer	53.8	15.4	38.5	69.2	7.7	7.7	53.8
		Supervision	Coping	Consulting	Prevention	Fit for Work	Communication Culture	Other
Perceived Goal Achievement (1 not at all, 5 extremely)	CISM	4.3	—	4.0	4.4	3.0	4.2	4.3
	Non-CISM	4.4	4.3	4.0	4.7	4.5	3.5	4.6
	Peer	4.9	5.0	4.2	4.8	5.0	4.4	4.3

Program (ASAP) produced not only the expected CISM benefits for the staff victims, but also an unexpected benefit of sharp reductions in violence. The overall benefit of CISM for the DFS and the controllers personally was estimated extremely high, even by the controllers of the non-CISM-group. Some participants of the non-CISM-group and some peers reported that CISM is regarded as a kind of back-up, which can be relied on in situations that are too difficult to cope with alone. From the peers' perspective, CISM created a better culture of error handling, trust, and more accessibility.

From other aviation studies (Kastner, Ademmer, et al, 1998; Kastner, Vogt, et al, 2000; Kastner, Köper, et al, 2002), it is suggested that appropriate culture and optimal leadership have the potential to increase job satisfaction significantly. The documented CISM-induced cultural improvements as well as the management's commitment to the program thus can be assumed to have systemic benefits for the DFS in general. The lack of acceptance of psychological and emotional factors at work, such as in the coping with critical incidents, are most frequently mentioned next to job organization, communication, and leadership as the most serious grievance by employees (Müller-Gethmann, et al, 2003). The findings of this study, as well as the results in the literature, show that although improvements in capacity and performance have typically been attempted with technical solutions, more money should be spent on human resources.

Certainly, the described effects are obvious, especially after accidents or critical incidents, but they also foster positive effects within the organization in general.

As goals of the DFS CISM program, the ATCOs primarily mentioned the enlargement of communication possibilities after critical incidents (supervision), whereas the peers emphasized the avoidance of long-term emotional consequences, which in the case of Post Traumatic Stress Disorder (PTSD) could lead to substantial loss of performance capability. The achievement of these DFS CISM objectives was estimated to be successful.

Lessons Learned

Due to apparent overall positive effects of the program, efforts for providing CISM services and comparable interventions should be supported throughout the flight safety field. Since the CISM- and non-CISM groups differed in their distress after the incident, the future strategy should be twofold. First, in order to include the non-CISM-group, the CISM intervention could be promoted as a tool for disseminating detailed information concerning the circumstances of an incident. Second, CISM could be utilized to decrease the culture of self-blame that often surrounds critical incidents in the ATC field. Since many controllers interpret critical incidents, such as separation loss, as a sign of failure and weakness, they are less likely to request a CISM intervention.

They might be more likely to participate, however, if the program also included detailed information about the incident and how to prevent it in the future. Since CISM was associated with economic savings in this sample, organizations should have an added incentive in enacting these programs.

References

Angenendt, A. (2003). Safety and security from the air traffic control services (ATCS) point of view. In J. Vogt & M. Kastner (Guest Eds.), Interfaces in air traffic organisation, Special Issue of the *Journal of Human Factors and Aerospace Safety, 3*, 207-209.

Boudreau, J. W. & Ramstad, P. M. (2003). Strategic industrial and organizational psychology and the role of utility analysis models. In W. C. Borman, D. R. Ilgen & R. J. Klimoski (Eds.), *Handbook of psychology: Vol. 12. Industrial and organizational psychology* (pp. 193-221). New York: John Wiley and Sons.

Brähler, E. & Scheer, J. W. (1983). *Der Gießener Beschwerdefragebogen (GBB)*. Stuttgart, Wien: Hans Huber.

Deuchert, I. & Eißfeld, H. (1998). Potenzialanalyse in der Flugsicherung. In M. Kleinmann & B. Strauße (Hrsg.), *Potenzialfeststellung und Personalentwicklung*. Göttingen: Verlag für Angewandte Psychologie.

Everly, G. S. (1999). A primer on Critical Incident Stress Management: What's really in a name. *International Journal of Emergency Mental Health, 1*, 76-78.

Everly, G. S. (2000). Five principles of crisis intervention: Reducing the risk of premature crisis intervention. *International Journal of Emergency Mental Health, 2*, 1-4.

Everly, G. S. & Mitchell, J. T. (1997). *Critical incident stress management: A new era and standard of care in crisis intervention*. Ellicott City, MD, USA: Chevron Publishing Corp.

Flannery, R. B., Jr. (1998). *The Assaulted Staff Action Programme (ASAP): Coping with the psychological aftermath of violence*. Ellicott City, MD, USA: Chevron Publishing Corporation.

Fleishman, E. A. & Reilly, M. E. (1992). *Handbook of human abilities—definitions, measurements and job task requirements*. Palo Alto, CA, USA: Consulting Psychologists Press.

Kastner, M., Ademmer, C., Budde, G., Hagemann, T., Udovic, A. & Vogt, J. (1998). *Belastung und Beanspruchung in den Flugsicherungsdiensten*. Arbeitswissenschaftliches Gutachten an die DFS. Offenbach: Deutsche Flugsicherung.

Kastner, M., Köper, B., Hagemann, T., & Hein, M. (2002). *Belastung und Beanspruchung in der Vorfeldkontrolle. Arbeitswissenschaftliches Gutachten an die Fraport AG*. Frankfurt: Fraport AG.

Kastner, M., Vogt, J., Köper, B., Udovic, A., & Hagemann, T. (2000). *Belastung und Beanspruchung in den Flugsicherungsdiensten AIS, FDB und FIS*. Arbeitswissenschaftliches Gutachten an die DFS. Offenbach: Deutsche Flugsicherung.

Kirkpatrick, D. (1994). *Evaluating training programs: The four levels*. San Francisco: Barrett-Koehler.

Krauth, J. (1988). Distribution-free statistics: An application-oriented approach. In J. P. Huston (Ed.), *Techniques in the behavioral and neural sciences, Vol. 2* (p. 37). Amsterdam: Elsevier.

Mitchell, J. T. & Everly, G. S. (2001). *Critical Incident Stress Debriefing: An Operations Manual for CISD, Defusing and Other Group Crisis Intervention Services* (3rd ed.). Ellicott City, MD, USA: Chevron Publishing Corp.

Müller-Gethmann, H., Bindzius, F., Bochmann, F., Boege, K., Hanßen-Pannhausen, R., Schmidt, N. & Windemuth, D. (2003). Psychological stress at work—scale, importance, and relevance for the companies. Paper presented at the symposium Emotions and Psychological Stress at Work, University of Dortmund.

Phillips, J. J. (1996, April). Measuring ROI: The 5th level of evaluation. *Technical and Skills Training*. Retrieved September 22, 2004, from www.astd.org/NR/rdonlyres/DOBCF259-880D-4EEC-BF89-7F1B9A88F430/0/phillips.pdf.

Rohrmann, B. (1978). Empirische Studien zur Entwicklung von Antwortskalen für die sozialwissenschaftliche Forschung. *Zeitschrift für Sozialpsychologie, 9*, 222-245.

Woldring, V. S. M. (1996). *Human Factors Module Stress*. HUM.ET1.ST13.2000-REP-01. Brussels: Eurocontrol.

Woldring, V. S. M. & Amat, A.-L. (1997). *Human Factors Module Critical Incident Stress Management*. HUM.ET1.ST13.3000-REP-01. Brussels: Eurocontrol.